No Purp

PTSD

Post-Traumatic Stress Disorder

Vietnam War Experiences

Larry Delong

Preface

At the tender age of 21, I was drafted into the US Army. During basic training, it was decided by the Army that my M.O.S. (Military-Occupational-Specialty) would be 11B infantry riflemen. I soon became an expert in many combat weapons, including the M-121 rifle, M-1 rifle, carbine rifle, and M-60 machine gun. I also went through eight weeks of advanced infantry drilling to be combat-ready. At the end of all this training, I felt macho, gung-ho, and highly patriotic. It wouldn't be long before all these mixed feelings and emotions would come into play.

In early October 1965, I got my orders to join the 1st Calvary Division to help support the war effort in South Vietnam. This infantry division was the first airmobile unit in the Army. It represented a new approach and innovation to infantry tactics.

While enjoying this book, you'll be amazed at what the human brain and body can endure when tested to its ultimate limitations. I intend to show the reader my endurance, from fighting in the jungles of Vietnam for 6 1/2 months to recovering in numerous hospitals worldwide for 7 1/2 months.

Dedication

This book is dedicated to my very good friend Dylan Wisdom who once again made this book possible to get published. His tireless effort was also the reason my first book was published, titled (It's Not Easy Being Me - Bar Hopping Thru Life). Thanks again, buddy, for all your hard work.

I also wish to extend this dedication to my two families, including my children, grandchildren, and great-grandchildren, along with my two ex-wives.

God Bless us all,

Larry Delong

Contents

Introduction

The title of this book is in no way implying or suggesting that such a prestigious medal as the Purple Heart be awarded to soldiers of war who have PTSD. Even today, 271,000 Vietnam soldiers are treated for this illness through medication and therapy. The whole intent of the title is to bring more attention and awareness to the seriousness of this mental and emotional condition caused by exposure to and experiencing life-threatening war events.

While surviving incredible and overwhelming obstacles in Vietnam, much later, I was also being treated for several ailments related to Vietnam. Yet it took 45 long, frustrating years for the doctors to diagnose my post-traumatic stress disorder. To all of that, I say at least I am still here.

We all owe a great deal of gratitude to all those who never made it back home to be reunited with their families and loved ones.

This feeling we all enjoy today, called freedom, is only made possible by the American soldier of today and throughout our country's history. To every day and last one of them, I only have one thing to say, "Thank You."

Chapter 1

PREPARING FOR WAR

After my infantry training, I was assigned to Fort Myer in Virginia to become a member of the Honor Guard at Arlington Cemetery. This outfit, along with all its shine, spit, and polish, is also an infantry unit. While performing daily ceremonial activities, you were also required to spend two weeks each summer at Fort Meade in Maryland to keep abreast of your infantry skills.

My honor guard specialty was participating in the 21-gun salute, a tradition performed at every funeral in Arlington. After several months of this trying and stressful duty, the army transferred me to Fort McNair in Washington, DC.

While there, I was assigned to the motor pool, and soon I was driving jeeps, trucks, bosses, and even their ambulance. I was quickly promoted to driving the staff cars for army officers and higher-ranking Sergeants. I'm sure my regimented spit and polishing training was why I was constantly requested as a driver for many staff cars.

My stay at Fort McNair would be short-lived as I was about to receive my new orders. Shortly before my new orders arrived, I was promoted to night dispatcher. This also meant my living quarters would be upstairs at the motor pool headquarters. I was responsible for dispatching all vehicles from 11:00 PM until 7:00 AM. Weeks passed, and my new orders hadn't arrived, and I was just constantly told that they were processing them and that I would be transferring out. At that point, I was still determining where or exactly when, but it would be soon. I was starting to enjoy and get accustomed to my new position, and a week later, my orders arrived.

I was reporting for work one evening, and the Sergeant in charge of the motor pool approached me and said that my transfer papers were there. As he handed them to me, he also stood there while I opened them up. As I read, he kept asking, where are they sending you? I answered in total shock to Vietnam.

My instant thought was that this was like reading my death sentence. Numerous stories on T.V. and read countless newspaper articles about Vietnam, and none of them had anything good to say. The orders read that I was to report to California in a few days for shipping overseas. I thought, hell no, I needed a couple of weeks to prepare physically and mentally.

Immediately, I was off to confront the company commander about allowing me a two-week leave to return home to visit family, relatives, and close friends. I explained to him that this could be my final goodbye to all my loved ones. I told him it would be inhumane to send me off to war without this opportunity, and surprisingly enough, he agreed. He told me he would do his best to alter the orders to allow me to go home and visit family. He told me to start packing and would let me know as soon as possible. I was already packed and anxiously waiting when the good news finally came down that all the orders stayed the same, except the dates were changed to allow me my two weeks' leave. Although I hadn't even started to leave, my mind was traveling one-hundred miles an hour. I had to squeeze in a lifetime of events in a few short weeks.

As my mind was racing, immediate preparation kept creeping to the forefront of my list of things to do. I kept asking myself, how do you prepare for jungle warfare? In all my infantry training, I couldn't remember anything explicit in that type of war, except my hand-to-hand combat could come into play. I had to prepare to leave Fort McNair and say my final goodbyes to my Army buddies and friends I made outside the military. I had two days to accomplish all this, and my flight home was already made.

I didn't have time to sell my 1954 Mercury automobile, so I told all my friends I would leave it on a nearby street with the keys and the signed registration in the glove compartment. The new owner would be the lucky person to first come across it. On the short flight home, I quickly made a mental list of people I had to see and spend some quality time with before flying off to war. The list consisted of family, relatives, friends, and my girlfriend, and we had decided to hold off our marriage until after my Army service.

I only had two short weeks before reporting to the West Coast to be shipped out to the war in Vietnam, so I was determined to make the most of every single day. My parents picked me up at the Buffalo airport, about forty minutes from our house. During the short drive home, it felt like 1000 questions were asked, primarily by my mother. They were concerned about my safety during the war and my future, which sounded like typical parents. At that point, I knew that I also had to mentally prepare them both in the upcoming days before my final departure.

During my short home visit, I tried to keep a positive attitude by avoiding newspapers and all T.V. news events. I portrayed this P.M.A., or positive mental attitude, with every individual I had the pleasure of spending time with. I knew that I was not on vacation but only on a mission. This mission was to instill tranquility and Peace of Mind in myself and all those who meant the world to me, like family, loved ones, and numerous friends.

I was tremendously busy scurrying around my hometown of Niagara Falls, NY. Still, I also found a few days to visit my brother and sister and their families in North Carolina. With this visitation completed along with Niagara Falls, my short-term goal of preparation was accomplished.

It was time to start preparing for my long-term goal: to stay alive during my tour in Vietnam. I kept a positive attitude about returning to these same great people. We had just shared stories and laughter and even embraced each other in tears. The day for departure had arrived, and I'd be heading back to the Buffalo airport to fly out to California to meet my deadline to report for my Vietnam tour of duty.

In the car driving back, it was my father, mother, and fiancé, Patricia. Unlike the previous trip, only a few words were spoken as everyone seemed to have a lot on their mind. This was the hardest goodbye I'd ever known, and as we departed, there wasn't a dry eye among us.

For the past few weeks, I was constantly surrounded day and night by loved ones, but now I was all alone to deal with my inner thoughts and emotions. I knew I was physically fit, but on the four-hour flight to the West Coast, I had to adjust my mind to war mode and get mentally fit. I was also aware that I wasn't going to Vietnam and sitting behind some desk, cooking in some mesh hall, or even being a clerk in the supply tent. I was going there to fight and engage in combat with the enemy.

I must admit that during the long flight, I had several negative thoughts, such as getting wounded, having parts of my body dismembered, yes, and even death. I also remember chanting silently in my mind, Vietnam ready or not, here I come.

I'm In Basic Training in the Year 1965.

Chapter II

MY NEW FAMILY IN ANKHE, VIETNAM

I was in its early stage when I first arrived. I immediately went through a thorough screening which took a few days. Along with all this screening, I was given all the supplies that the Army thought I would need and fit into my backpack.

I was then issued my new combat weapon, the M-16 rifle. I would learn quickly how to use it and adequately keep it clean. I was informed that this weapon must never be out of sight or leave my side. Then I was given enough ammunition that my gun belt Would carry, and I always found extra room in my backpack for a few additional ammo clips. Finally, I was told I would fly out by helicopter in the morning to join up with my new company in the jungle.

Out there, always somewhere in the jungle, I would meet up with what I considered my new family away from home. I didn't know then how close these family members would become. It soon became apparent that honesty and total trust were the order of the day.

The makeup of your company usually consisted of your Captain, four Lieutenants, four Sergeants, and four Platoons, consisting of anywhere from ten to fourteen soldiers. The company could have anywhere from fifty to seventy members at different times. You can understand why we were all on a just first-name basis. Your closest family members would be the members in your platoon, and you learned that you didn't keep any secrets from them and you could speak your mind. These family members you would patrol with every day and dig your foxhole with every night. At dusk, you got a fellow platoon member, and you would dig your two-man foxholes together. The platoon would create a circular perimeter as best as possible to prevent infiltrators.

The author Larry Delong at the age 21 in 1964, during boot camp.

Before dark, each foxhole would set up trip flares in front of their positions to alert them of any movement trying to enter our facility. Many times, these flares would be tripped by animals roaming around. Nonetheless, it would cause immense anxiety and trigger many rifles blazing away before they would get the order to cease fire. It always reminded you of that old phrase that it's better to be safe than sorry.

Many of my family members had nicknames for their M-16 rifles. I decided to call mine sweetheart to remind me of the one I left behind. During numerous firefights, I would constantly utter the words don't let me down now, sweetheart. I kept the hygiene of my sweetheart to the utmost highest level possible to ensure my safety and that of my family members. I saved as much food and ammunition as possible to keep her fed during any dire situation.

It had to be an extreme emergency to borrow water or ammunition from even one of your family members. These were the two most precious commodities you carried with your cans of ration for survival. To give up any one of these, it had to be beneficial to both parties involved.

At times, the jungle was so thick and dense that it took several days to get supplies dropped in by helicopter, like cans of food, water, and ammo. This was just one reason your family members were so stingy with their survival items. If your lucky stars were perfectly in line, you could receive all three precious essentials in one helicopter drop. Usually, it took several days in between to receive all three.

Each company had its medic and, if possible, an army chaplain. I never saw the medic hold a rifle, and when I asked him about it, he just smiled and said I'm here to save lives, not take them. He simply carried a small firearm on his hip for his protection. Most of the equipment he carried was medical supplies. I always had the greatest respect for our medic and hoped I wouldn't need any of his attention. You could be sure of one thing if you did need his service, you would not be getting a bill in the mail later.

Another critical position in our company was the machine gunner. We would carry a M-50 along with a M-60 machine gunner. These gunners could clear out an area in minutes and supply excellent cover during a heavy attack. Our company also consisted of a very efficient person handling the M-79 grenade launcher. This weapon also reminded me of a sawed-off shotgun. It could launch grenades in a far distance and reach towering trees, which came in handy to remove hiding snipers in them.

I felt very proud of my new family and highly secure. My new family was made up of different religions, races, and beliefs. Everyone was treated as an equal, and no matter what, no type of discrimination ever surfaced. Everybody in the platoon selected a partner they thought they would feel comfortable with. This partner would help dig and share your foxhole every night. You would soon bond a special trust in this person.

Every foxhole had its own rules and hours of watch time at night. The main thing was that the foxhole had to be awake and alert all night. Even in my foxhole, the hours and times would change due to daily circumstances. While digging my foxhole every night, the thought that this could be my grave would also creep into my mind.

I and my partner most nights would share our foxhole with some very uncomfortable and unwanted guests. Even if it was your time to rest, various crawling and biting critters often awakened you. No matter how big or bad the bite, you knew that making any sound was out of the question. You tried to squash it with your hand and wait till daylight to examine your prey.

From the time you started digging your foxhole, which is usually about dusk, there was no light allowed, including smoking cigarettes. Even a lit cigarette could be seen for miles in total darkness of the mountainous jungles of Vietnam. The restriction of any light or fire after dusk also would pertain to the use of the sterno pill that you used to heat all your cans of C-ration food. This meant that you ate those meals cold and greasy most mornings and evenings.

To feast upon these so-called delicious and nutritious cans of food, the Army supplied most boxes of canned meals with a P-38 can opener. It was very small and flat but fast and efficient at opening any size or type of can. You had to dispose of your cans by digging a small hole and burying them.

This was done to prevent the Vietcong soldiers from finding them and making weapons out of them. They would use them to make bombs and mines, shape the metal, and sharpen it to a razor finish. With the lack of materials, they were inventive in making weaponry out of crude and ordinary items.

Early 1960's Map of combat forces in South Vietnam. I was with the First Cavalry in Ankhe.

Chapter III

POISON BAMBU STICKS

Whether as a squad, platoon, or company, we were on the move every single day. If you held the rank lower than a Sergeant, you were never informed of your destination. You were only given directions such as straight ahead, back up, or left and right turn. So, at the end of the day, you never know whether you reached your destination. At no time did you even know where you were. Well, it really didn't matter. You only knew you were done tramping through the jungle because you just got the order to form a perimeter and start digging your foxhole. Sometimes after you dug your foxhole and set up your flares, you got the order that we were moving out, and the choppers would be there in twenty minutes. It didn't matter where you were going to be dropped off. It only meant the digging of another foxhole. I soon learned there were two types of war, daytime and nighttime, and I didn't care much for either.

The Vietcong soldier went by the nickname of Charlie and was innovative in inventing cheap methods of slowing and even stopping our troops' movements. One unique weapon, known as the pungi stick, consisted of branches of bamboo that were sharpened at both ends to a razor point. At one end, the bamboo would be smeared with human feces, while the other end would be used to stick in the ground. These sticks would be scattered over mountainsides and thick brush, and just about anywhere that grass was ankle to chest high. These pungi sticks aimed not to kill the American soldier but to wound them so that he would be evacuated and hospitalized. These sticks were so strong and sharp that they cut through leather like a hot knife into butter.

The choppers were forever picking us up and dropping us off at all hours of the day, as this was the case one morning, even before we could enjoy our cold, greasy breakfast. We were informed that we were heading to support another company that got hit hard the night before and sustained several injuries and a few casualties.

As the choppers dropped us off, everyone scrambled for some cover. The entire company was unloaded in about ten minutes. It wasn't long until we heard several screens of agony. Immediately we saw the medic running past everyone toward the chilling sounds. It wasn't long after that it became silent, meaning the medic had done his job temporarily.

Word returned to us that two soldiers had run into those pungi sticks. One was from a different squad, and the other was from our unit. I talked to this soldier several times, and he told me that he was just a young country boy and was still looking to visit the big city someday.

Two helicopters were called back to Medevac, the two wounded, and it only took about 10 minutes for them to arrive. They landed in a clearing nearby, and I could see them loading the stretchers onto the choppers. Both individuals were waving goodbye to their comrades. Also, I'm sure we were all praying for their health and well-being. At the same time, I was also hoping that the young country boy would get his wish and someday get to visit a big city.

Word came a little later: one soldier was wounded in the stomach, and the other young man from our squad was injured in the leg. It seemed that the pungi stick had punctured through his boot and ran into his leg. Soon we were told we could chow down as we would leave the area later in the day. Since the site was saturated with pungi sticks, I'm sure it had something to do with the decision to leave the area.

A short time later, I saw a swarm of choppers in the sky looking for a place to land near our position. Choppers were here to move us to a new location. They intended to move both companies out of the area to a new, unknown location. For a week or a little more, we were constantly on maneuvers with no significant events other than cutting through thick brush and entangled vines and climbing hilly terrains.

We were on patrol for about two hours after breakfast a short time later when we all heard someone holler for the medic. At that time, we were all in a single line, and the voice came from near the front of the line. Within seconds, I saw the medic whizzing past me with total disregard for his own safety. Shortly after he arrived at the wounded soldier, the loud moaning sounds ceased.

We all froze to await further orders and try to find out what was happening. Word finally came down the line that another one of our platoon members had run into a pungi stick that had pierced his stomach. We were told that the medic was patching him up, and we were waiting for a chopper to evacuate him.

About ten minutes later, we heard the chopper in the air, and we were told it was looking for a safe place to land because of the pungi sticks. Finally, it landed several hundred feet behind our line. They had to carry the wounded soldier by stretcher the entire way. As he was being carried past us, you could see his bandaged stomach, which was already bloody. He was constantly talking to the medic, as I could hear several times, and answering the medic. Are we there yet? I could also hear the medic reply almost, soldier, almost. Just before they loaded them into the chopper, he picked up his head and smiled while giving us all the thumbs up.

Chapter IV

A FOXHOLES VIEW

Being in the infantry in the army never presented a problem for me until I was sent to Vietnam. I soon discovered that I was spending 1/3 of my entire time there living in a foxhole. The depth you and your partner would dig your bed for the night depended on the terrain. You never knew what would come crawling into your foxhole at night to share and enjoy the luxury of your sleeping quarters.

You tried to get a little shut eye when you were not on watch. Sleeping with one eye open almost became a reality in Vietnam when you were out in the jungles. The slightest sound would cause you to open both eyes to look around and observe the surroundings. Sometimes you would wake to check on your partner in the foxhole, ensuring he was also awake and watching.

The nights always seemed long, while your sleep was amazingly short. What the human body can get used to when pushed to its limits is incredible. During extreme distress, no matter your religion, you seemed to turn to your God for help. War has this kind of effect on individuals of every faith. Every night while I was sitting in my foxhole, I would ask my God to help me make it through the night, and at the start of every day, I would repeat the prayer for that day.

Vietnam had a very extended rainy season, and often at night, your foxhole would become a wading pool. Also, you became accustomed to sitting in water and sleeping in the rain. On most rainy days or nights, you almost enjoy it, as this was the only shower you would get. I've been here in Vietnam for over a month and was still looking for a regular bath or shower. If we were crossing some body of water, we would dip as low as possible to bathe and clean our clothes. The only thing that stayed dry was your weapon.

Your hygiene had to take a back seat to your safety and survival. When you did have a chance to brush your teeth and rinse your mouth, you used only a tiny sip of water. Water was like liquid gold. Next to your weapon, water was a primary source for your survival. If possible, choppers would drop a giant rubber water ball in our area every few days, so we all could fill our canteens with water.

You could never imagine the great feeling you would have after filling your canteens with water and having plenty of ammunition on your gun belt and in your backpack. It felt like you just got a raise in pay on your job, and it was payday. It was amazing how the little things in life became so crucial in Vietnam during the war. Your looks and attire weren't on your priority list of things to do. I carried a comb, but it was never used due to its filthy condition. I would just run my fingers through my hair and slap my head on my head.

While water was a primary source of survival, you also had to eat every day. Our boxes of c-rations also would be delivered by choppers every few days. You would take these cans of food and stuff them into your extra pair of socks and tie them to your belt or backpack. Although this was a convenient way of carrying your food, it wasn't a practical way to travel through the jungles.

You would be carrying enough cans of food in your socks for at least two or three days. Each sock would hold at least five cans of food so that the sock would stretch to almost two feet long. While stomping and trampling through the thick brush, these long dangling socks of food would get tangled on every vine, twig, branch, and even small bushes. It would be up to the person in line behind you to untangle the mess and set you free.

Before you retired to your foxhole for the night, you tried to make sure that your bathroom activities were finished for the night. Taking a piddle during the day or night was not a problem, but taking a poop could be, especially at night. Every time you engage in a crap day or night, a hole must be dug so the feces can be buried.

This wasn't done because of the smell or being worried that someone might step in it. The sole reason was if the Vietcong soldiers found the feces, it could be used to dip their pungi sticks in and be more poison weapons used against the American soldiers that would follow.

No matter how busy or exhausting your activities were during the day, it seemed you always looked forward to sitting in that foxhole at night to let your mind and body relax. For some unknown reason, the whole damn war looked so different during the total darkness of the night while you watched from the foxhole.

While you were constantly observing your surroundings, your mind, and thoughts would wander about loved ones and family back home. During the peace and quiet of the night, you couldn't help but let your mind wander about happier thoughts of home.

Yet the mind would also reflect on all the activities during the day. Each day seemed endless as you had to be constantly on alert, and your mind didn't have time to wander. Letting your mind wander during the day could be very dangerous to yourself and others around you. Believe it or not, you felt safe in your foxhole during the night because it became your only fortress during your entire day.

Chapter V

VISITING BASE CAMP

In over six months of my Vietnam tour of duty, I could only remember visiting my base camp on two occasions, and neither resulted in taking a shower. Word came down the line that we would return to base camp in a couple of days.

The reason for the return was to freshen up, clean your weapons thoroughly and take time to relax. For a change, you would be out of the weather in a huge canvas tent, which meant getting the chance to sleep on a cot. The thought of taking a shower was foremost and utmost on your mind. At this point, you weren't informed how long our stay would be at camp.

Finally, the morning after breakfast, the word came that the choppers would be here shortly to take us back to base camp. We were told to gather all our belongings and prepare for the choppers. This also meant cleaning up the immediate area. We heard the choppers approaching, and you could instantly see smiles on everybody's faces.

This was the first time I saw smiles on faces at the sound of choppers approaching because it usually meant that we were heading into some trouble. Once entering the choppers, it was a delightful thirty-minute ride back to base camp. The landing field was just on the outskirts of our camp, about a twenty-minute march to our area. We were told to file a single line at the end of the airstrip to march into our headquarters proudly.

On the short march, we passed by tents that rear-echelon soldiers occupied. These soldiers were not in the infantry and had other duties that required them to stay in base camp. This meant they enjoyed all the hospitalities the camp had to offer daily.

The benefits included more than just sleeping off the ground in an entirely closed structure and eating three hot meals daily. The showers were available to them whenever they needed or wanted. I heard that movies were also shown at night for their entertainment. They were shopping daily at the base store to replenish goods they used regularly, like soap, deodorant, toothpaste, shampoo, and mouthwash, to mention a few.

Halfway through our march to reach our area, one of these rear-echelon individuals stood outside his tent, taking pictures of us filing by. I guess I just snapped as I ran towards the soldier, knocked him to the ground, and sent his camera flying and landing several feet from him. While he was on the ground yelling obscenities at me, I was jumping and stopping on his camera. I finally kicked it and sent it flying again. Now, all I had in my mind was to kick the soldier's ass. My Sergeant grabbed me by the arm and said that's enough, soldier; get back in line, and we will deal with this later. When we started to march on, I could still hear the soldier hollering that I would pay for this. This was the last thing on my mind at this particular time.

While I was getting back in line, I hollered back to the soldier. If you want to see fighting men or action, grab your damn weapon, if you can find it, and follow us back into the thick of the jungles. We were told from the beginning that the two things you never packed when going out in the jungle on patrol were a portable radio or any camera. They explained that both items could get you or your fellow soldiers killed.

Most of our patrols were held to a low whisper, and we were in total silence when moving at night. The higher echelon feared that if cameras were taken out into the jungles, some soldiers might be taking pictures of wounded or dead individuals. Some of them might even be our soldiers. The mental images you can't help but develop in your mind will last you your entire life.

We finally reached our tent, and I made it to my cot and decided to sit and relax for a few minutes before my shower. I still thought the military police would enter my tent and arrest me for my previous action. My Sergeant entered my tent a short time later and told me that everything was taken care of, and I was to try and control my temper in the future. I thanked him and started getting ready for that long-awaited and overdue shower.

As I was removing my socks, I was in total shock. My feet were as black as coal, and my skin looked flaky. I immediately hollered to my Sergeant to come and look. He ordered me to put my boots back on and get my ass to the medic tent pronto.

The medic tent was only a few tents over from mine. I was sitting there and waiting for medical attention within ten minutes. The medic was another Sergeant in rank, so I at least knew that he had some previous medical experience. After discussing why I was there, he told me to remove my boots and socks. Once removed, he instantly stood up and started some vulgar language describing the condition of my feet. He ended by asking me how in the hell I let my feet get this bad. I could see that it was obvious that he didn't have a damn clue about the living conditions out there in the jungle. I distinctly remember him shouting that my feet were the worst case of the jungle rot that he had ever seen.

I was getting upset with his choice of words and demeanor. It spontaneously Turned into a shouting match between us, both standing face to face. I tried to remember what happened a short time ago, and my Sergeant told me about my temper. I'm sure these thoughts kept me from punching him squarely in the jaw. The shouting and language were getting so loud it brought an officer scampering from the back of the tent to investigate what was happening.

With an immediate threat from the officer of having me locked up in the guardhouse for insubordination, I suddenly shut my mouth, came to attention, and saluted. The officer stated that since no punches were thrown, this could be worked out to everyone's benefit. He told the medic to give me all the proper medication and instructions for applying it.

The medic started gathering different solutions and creams and instructed me on all their proper uses and how often. I immediately asked him about a shower, and he said empathetically and absolutely not. He instructed me to return to my tent and start soaking my feet in one of the solutions that he gave me. He stated that he was trying to save my feet and that I didn't realize how bad they were. He also suggested I sponge bath the best I could while in my tent. I decided to take his advice and hope for the best. I couldn't help thinking that I had only been in base camp for about four hours and already got into two skirmishes.

I was smiling and just thinking I was doing a lot better in the jungles. Surely, but slowly, all the happy thoughts I brought to the base camp were shrinking away by the hour. Because of the condition of my feet, my remaining meals were brought into my tent, almost like room service. The supper was the last meal delivered, along with bad news; it was for dessert. The news was we were moving back out into the jungles in the morning and to get all our gear clean and ready tonight. The medic cleared me with instructions to continue with his medications and to rejoin my company.

The following morning, I was standing alert and ready on the base airfield with all my clean gear and medication. I was wondering what the hell was next, like the old saying that all is fair in love and war, which I have heard many times. At this point, I was looking for a bit of love.

Chapter VI

MINES AND EXPLOSIVES

After our short stay at base camp, we were off to another unknown location in the midst of the jungles. Even as brief a stay, I felt refreshed and eager to meet the challenging days ahead. My main concern at this time was not only to stay alive but also to save and keep my feet. I remembered the medics' orders and intended to abide by them as much as possible.

After about a forty-five-minute ride in the choppers, they were looking for a clearing to land safely. It seemed like caution was foremost rather than urgency for a change. Once we landed and gathered on the ground at the company, we were told to line up as we were prepared to patrol the area for a few hours before we would make camp for the night.

The jungle area was mildly thick; in some areas, we had to use our machetes to advance our progress. Every soldier carried this long-bladed knife. This machete looked like a version of a short sword. Besides being used periodically to help clear your way, it could be used very effectively in hand-to-hand combat.

We were soon told that we were trying to make it into a clearing a short distance away so the choppers could pick us up to take us to another destination. About an hour later, we reached this clearing, finding the choppers were already there, waiting. We immediately hopped aboard, and we were off to who knows where.

We were on the choppers for about twenty minutes before we started to land near a road with several army trucks waiting for us. Once we were all on the ground, they told us to load up in the trucks, and they would drive us down the road to our new location. While riding in the back of the truck, I started thinking that just driving down an actual paved road was the most civilization I had seen in almost two months. It sure felt good while it lasted.

About thirty minutes into the ride, the trucks pulled off the road, and we were told to jump off and line up in a single file. We were about to go on patrol again. We started across this field, which you could see ahead was nothing but a jungle. Less than five minutes into our patrol, we all heard a loud explosion and saw a body ahead of us flip up in the air; immediately, moans and screams came from that area. We were all instructed not to take another step and freeze in place. We all knew that somebody had stepped on a mine. The adrenaline was flowing overtime.

Looking down the line, I could see about a dozen soldiers ahead of me, the individual lying on the ground with his leg twisted behind him. The leg was blown off from the knee and only held on by a few ligaments. By this time, the medic was by his side, giving him first aid. He hollered out that he needed a stretcher, and soon the soldier was running past us with one.

Knowing the circumstances, I gave a lot of credit to this brave soldier. They were soon lagging him on the stretcher with the best of care as not to detach his leg. The clearing was behind us, so that was where the chopper was already landing. I hoped they could get him aboard the chopper without stepping on another mine. As they carried him past us, I could hear him repeatedly saying, at least I'm going home.

Every soldier in line shouted out best wishes and good luck to a full recovery. There was a thumbs up and reply, God bless us all because we would need it. I could hear those words as clearly today as I did back then.

The chopper finally lifted off, and we wondered what the hell was next. We were immediately ordered to turn around in place and backtrack on the same path to the main road that we just entered the field.

The truck convoy was already called back to take us to another location. As we were all aboard the trucks and riding down the highway, I was sure we all were thinking of the unfortunate soldier we just left behind. I especially kept thinking about the words he left us with, "God bless us all as we were going to need it." Those very words would haunt me during my entire time in Vietnam.

About thirty minutes into our convoy ride to a new location, we all heard a loud explosion. We were ordered to dismount the trucks and take cover. Word came quickly that one of the supply trucks had run over a mine in the road. We soon learned that the two passengers in the truck were fine, but the truck was disabled. Fortunately, it was only a supply truck and different from the truck we were in carrying a group of soldiers. This convoy would be delayed most of the day, so the choppers were called for us.

When the choppers arrived, the convoy personnel were sweeping the road for other mines, which would take significant time. The disabled truck had to be unloaded, and all the supplies were transferred to other trucks. By now, we were all on our way to another unknown location.

Chapter VII

TURKEY DAY AT CAMP

Other than the problem with the mines in the road, it sure was exciting seeing and traveling on a paved road. Although it didn't last long, it gave me hope that there is some type of civilization out there. It's amazing the simple things you miss in your everyday life, like roads, sidewalks, street signs, stop lights, and, yes, even traffic. We take hundreds of little things for granted, and living in these dense jungles does not offer any of those luxuries.

Yes, once again, the choppers dropped us off in some jungle area. At least for now, we weren't heading into any battle we knew of. For the next several days, we were only fighting the terrain, heat, bugs, critters, and even leeches. When we passed through a damp or swampy area, these parasites or so-called leeches would find their way into your boots and clothing.

These leeches had suckers on both ends of their bodies, so it was very easy for them to latch on to you once they were on your body. Once you discover a leech, you must get them off as soon as possible before they suck too much blood. The head of the reach is usually buried into your skin, and that part must be pulled away quickly. The point of entry will usually bleed for several minutes after this occurs. While throwing the leech to the ground and stepping on it, you'll see a large amount of blood squirting from its body.

Another blood-sucking parasite we were fighting was ticks. This little parasite would attach to you and immediately start sucking your blood. This critter would cause discomfort and pain. Both the leech and the tick, once removed, the area had to be treated with rubbing alcohol and a bandage. These two items were always carried in your backpack.

Holidays had little meaning here in the jungles, and there was no way to celebrate them anyway. We just simply and quietly celebrated each day you survived. We all knew that Thanksgiving was only three days away. I started thinking about my holiday meal and checked my cans of C-rations for the festive day.

As I was reading the labels on the canned, I couldn't even fantasize about anything that reminded me of the traditional Thanksgiving dinner. I looked at spaghetti and meatballs, ham and lima beans, ham and eggs, franks and beans, and various cans of crackers and desserts. If we didn't get a replenishment of rations in the next few days, I would have to choose between one of these delicacies. The main holiday course didn't matter as much, that I would still be alive to enjoy it. My motto was to live one day at a time and hope and pray to see the next.

While having one of our delicious breakfast meals the following day, we all received some good and bad news simultaneously. The good news was that we were flying back to base camp in two days to enjoy Thanksgiving dinner. The bad news was that we were not going to spend the night. The bad news didn't matter, as the good news was more than overwhelming. The other part of the good news was that we could wash up, as a full shower was out of the question. We would have time to get a clean change of clothes and adequately replenish our ammunition. The greatest news was that we would enjoy a complete and hot Thanksgiving dinner without worrying about getting fired upon.

I was already starting to be thankful for the many blessings during my stay in Vietnam up to this point. At the same time, I felt remorse for my fellow comrades that hadn't made it this far. I remember telling a fellow soldier one day as he was sitting around and just complaining about everything. Several of our comrades are no longer with us and just be grateful that he was still here to be able to complain.

I was politely telling him to shut his mouth because things could be a whole lot worse. He got the message because he looked at me with a blank expression on his face and never said another word. All my thoughts were on Thanksgiving dinner at base camp, and I was looking forward to it as a child would anticipate Christmas morning. I kept visualizing this dinner in my mind over and over for the next two days, to the point that I could almost smell and taste it.

Finally, the day arrived, and the choppers were here to take us to base camp. I was never so happy to see these choppers since I've been in Vietnam. The flight back to base camp lasted about 30 minutes and was relaxing. I couldn't help thinking we would fly back out later in the day. I could put that thought on hold for now as dinner was on my mind.

Once we landed, we got our instructions and orders for the day. We were told that there would be some reporters and photographers during dinner and that we would not have any dismission with them. If they approached us, we were to send them to our superiors.

The other order for the day was to clean up and look our best during dinner, and it was also stated that there would be cold bottles of beer being served with the meal. We were also ordered one beer per person as we were leaving shortly after dinner. It was very apparent to me that we were only brought out of the fields for this dinner to be part of a photo shoot for the news.

At the time, I was feeling used and disappointed. Then I looked around at all these happy and smiling faces I hadn't seen since I'd been here. I said to myself oh, what the hell, whatever it took to achieve this moment was well damn worth it. Tomorrow we will all be back in the thick of those dreary jungles and back to more serious business. I was more than willing to live for the moment.

During advanced infantry jungle training in 1965

Chapter VIII

IT JUST WASN'T MY TIME

When the choppers dropped us off, it looked like a very thick jungle area at the base of some very treacherous mountains. The orders came down that we would patrol the area and work our way up the hillside. As rough and thick as the terrain was, this was better than the minefields I had just left.

As we ascended the hillside, the environment got clearer, and the going got easier after several hours of patrol. We finally reached a level plateau. We got orders to relax, take off our gear, and enjoy our evening meal.

At the time, we were curious if it was just a supper break or if we would dig in for the night. It didn't matter; we were exhausted from the day's activities. It felt good to relax, enjoy a meal and worry about our next move later. We were finishing our evening meal and thinking about digging in for the night when the word came down from our Lieutenant to get all our gear together and be ready to move out.

Our Sergeant told us that another company not too far away was getting their asses kicked, and we would support them. The sarge also said to us that the choppers were already on their way to get prepared and check our ammunition. As the choppers approached, the butterflies in my stomach started churning.

Soon we are in the choppers and on our way to help this other company out of their dilemma. While sitting in the chopper where everyone was quiet and had a blank look on their face. Knowing that we were heading into a firefight, you couldn't help wondering if this would be the battle that your number might be called. Thinking of that, your greatest thought was to help out your fellow soldiers.

As we approached one area to land, we could hear the repeating sounds of gunfire. Looking around, all you could see was jungle and rice paddies. The chopper pilot hollered that it was too dangerous to land, so that he would fly in as low as possible, and we would have to jump out and roll on the ground. This exit from the chopper would be in the middle of the rice field.

Once this feat was performed and we were all on the ground, we crawled to the nearest rice bunker for shelter. We were fortunate on the landing not to have a single injury or casualty. When we were all in place, the word came down the line not to fire unless we were fired upon, as we had a patrol out in the jungle trying to return to our perimeter.

The brush ahead of us was very thick, but we could still hear several sounds of gunfire. About an hour had passed when we finally got the word that the platoon was about to enter our area and to make sure that nobody fired a shot. A short time later, the entire platoon was back inside our perimeter.

It wasn't long before the order came down to dig in for the night because we were sending out a patrol tomorrow to scout the area. With all the excitement going on, I never noticed that somewhere along the way, I lost both of my socks of food. My partner assured me he would help me out as he had more than enough until we replenished.

We both started to dig our foxhole, which was on the corner of the rice field. We didn't have to dig too far down because we would hit the water by digging a few feet down, and with the mound of dirt surrounding the field, it was ample enough shelter. But we both enjoyed the comfort of our dig. My Sergeant came over and told me I had to go on the pig patrol tonight.

The pig patrol consisted of two men sneaking outside the perimeter before dark for early detection of any infiltration during the night. One man would also carry a radio on his back to alert the people back inside the perimeter of any intruders. The two men would crawl back as fast as possible if this alert happened to rejoin everyone inside the perimeter. The name was chosen as you were thought of as a guinea pig for any intruders during the night.

Nothing happened this night, and we radioed in that we were returning to the perimeter. Once back inside the perimeter, I was told we would be there most of the day. I told my Sergeant I was expecting my foxhole back that I helped dig that night. He had taken over my foxhole with my partner while he sent me out on pig patrol. He told me and my radioman I spent the night with to dig another new foxhole. He pointed out a spot about six feet next to my previous foxhole.

I remember arguing about going on the pig patrol because I told him it wasn't my turn. I lost that argument simply because he reminded me about his rank. I was about to get into another very heated and cursing discussion with my Sergeant one more time. I knew this would be a losing battle but getting it off my chest felt good.

My radio man and I started to dig a foxhole next to him while I was constantly and quietly cursing him under my breath. Once our new foxhole was completely dug, we sat back and opened some cold breakfast c-rations. Shortly after breakfast, we sent out a squad of fellow soldiers to scout the immediate area. About an hour into their patrol, they started receiving gunfire.

We got word back that they were totally outmanned and were making their way back to the perimeter. We were told to hold fire until our squad safely returned to our area. Once the squad entered our perimeter, our headquarters had already called in for mortar support in our vicinity.

Instantly we could hear the mortar rounds exploding all around us. It sounded like the 4th of July without the fireworks. Explosions were so close to us that they made us all bury our heads face down in our foxholes. Explosions continued for about twenty minutes. At the end of all the noise, we all peeked our heads up and started looking around.

To my astonishment, as I looked over to my old foxhole, I observed only the remains of my Sergeant and my foxhole partner. They were both blown apart, and various parts of their bodies were scattered over two rice fields. While the medic was gathering their body parts, I couldn't help thinking this was the same foxhole I was arguing to get back a few hours ago.

I was sitting in my new foxhole in total shock and disbelief. I was mentally trying to digest the horrific events during the last few hours. I couldn't help but observe the medic gathering some of their body parts and placing them into body bags. This was the same foxhole I was arguing and ready to fight over earlier during the day. Little did I know at the time of this episode that it would cause me nightmares until this very day.

Very shortly, the gunfire started again, and we were busy exchanging fire aimlessly into the thickness of the jungle. Within minutes we could see rocket-firing gunships flying overhead and bombarding the entire area. This relentless assault would continue for at least thirty minutes. We could see trees and debris blowing up high in the air as the entire jungle area in front of us was leveled before our eyes. When the gunships finally left the area, it suddenly became very quiet.

We were all instructed to stop firing our weapons and remain in our foxholes. We were also informed that a small scouting patrol was being sent to evaluate the situation. While this small patrol was out scouting the area, we were left in our foxholes to contemplate the day's activities. At this time, my main concern was that there would be a recurrence of the day's action. I knew, at this point, everybody was mentally and physically exhausted.

It wasn't long before the patrol returned, and the word was the area was cleared out and numerous dead bodies observed. The word was that we would leave the area shortly and ensure you had all your gear together. While we were waiting, the soldier brought a piece of burnt flesh and hair that resembled someone's head. It belonged to one of the soldiers in the foxhole next to me.

With tears in his eyes, the soldier walked over to the medic and said, please make sure this head gets in the right body bag. The medic replied to the soldier that he could be sure of that. The first choppers that came into the area were to take the wounded and dead out. A short time later, several choppers arrived to take the remainder of us once again to a new location.

We got the news a few days later that a mortar round had landed in the foxhole next to me and blew the two individuals over two rice fields. Unfortunately, the two soldiers absorbed the total impact and just covered me and my buddy in the next foxhole with dirt and pieces of their flesh. Knowing from the beginning that it was my foxhole and the circumstances that followed, I came to only one conclusion. It just wasn't my time.

Chapter IX

TEMPORARY INSANITY

When walking or trying to make it through the tangling vines of the jungle, word would come down the line to stop and take a breather. This break could be anywhere from ten to twenty minutes long. Some soldiers would puff on a cigarette if they had them, and others would take a few minutes to sit and contemplate. It felt great to let your mind wander and escape the war, even briefly.

My escape moments always drifted back home to family and loved ones. I would think about the peace, quiet, and safe feeling you always remember, thoughts of when and even if you would see them all again. These precious moments didn't come that often during the daytime but were usually reserved for the lonely and quiet hours at night while sitting in your foxhole. Your secret war escape would soon be interrupted by the words we're moving out.

We were moving out after a short break. About one hour into our patrol, movement was suddenly stopped by gunfire. We all scrambled to take some cover. With the sound of gunfire, we could hear twigs and branches snapping around us. We got word that one or more snipers were in the immediate area. We were returning fire in the direction and area we thought the sounds were coming from. We soon heard they would blow the snipers out of the trees with our grenade launchers.

At the same time, we were getting gunfire from our left flank. The firing from the front came very sporadic and higher up. All the firing from the left was heavy and steady. There was no doubt in anyone's mind, and at this point, they had our entire platoon pinned down.

Since we had recently lost our Sergeant, we had a new and lot younger Sergeant acting as squad leader. I knew from the start that he was very ambitious and gung-ho. Where the fire was coming from on your left was higher up on the ridge. It was constant, and now it was lasting for about thirty minutes.

The front of the patrol was busy with the sniper or snipers as they were also pinned down. The firing from our left side took a few minutes pause, and I could see my Sergeant was getting very anxious to do something. The Sergeant whispered to me that he saw activity at the top of the hill and was trying his best to get me focused on the area. He instructed me to put a double clip of ammo in my weapon. When he moved out toward the hill I was to follow, I repeatedly fired my weapon toward the area he pointed out.

He also told me to pass the same word to the rest of our squad. I turned around and whispered the exact orders that my Sergeant gave to me. The next order was let's go and keep firing your weapon as you started charging up the hill. I was steadily behind him, firing in the direction I was told. As I was following my Sergeant and advancing up the hill, I looked behind me, and not a single person from our squad was following.

My adrenaline flowed over time as I was caught up in the moment. I was beginning to wonder if I was on a suicide mission. By now, I knew it was up to me and my Sarge to try and make it thru. More than halfway up the hill, we realized that the firing from above had ceased. We could now see a structure that looked like a man-made bunker.

The Sarge whispered to me that we were about 100 feet from the bunker, and then he had an insane moment of the two of us to stand up and keep firing as we approached the bunker. I must have had a John Wayne moment as I agreed, and we both stood up, firing away. Now we were standing almost side by side with our rifles blaring away until we reached the top of the bunker.

We looked over and into the bunker. We were amazed that no one, alive or dead, was there. As the stars that we were, we looked at each other and just smiled while engaging in the warmest handshake that I ever experienced. We realized then that this special bond between us would last forever.

The Sergeant promptly whistled and waved to the rest of the squad that climbed the hill and met us at the bunker. While waiting for our comrades to climb the hill, the Sarge observed and took inventory of all the belongings left behind.

The rest of our squad had finally caught up with us at the top of the hill; they were excited and wondering what the hell just happened. They claim that they never heard the order to follow up the ridge. They also informed us that the platoon had blown two snipers out of the trees, and we were ready to move out.

Just about that time, the Lieutenant was making his way up the hill toward us. He was not wearing a happy expression on his face. When he approached the squad leader, he started by saying you better start explaining what in the hell just happened. That was the question everyone had, including me.

After the Sergeant was thoroughly interrogated for about twenty minutes, it seemed like the Lieutenant had some strong mixed emotions. At one point, the Lieutenant was praising the both of us for our extreme bravery and almost sounded like he might even recommend us for some medal. Then the next moment, he was chewing us a new asshole. He even threatened us with a court martial for insubordination and leaving a company while under attack.

I couldn't help thinking this was twice I'd been threatened with a possible court martial in just the last couple of months. The Lieutenant finally ordered everyone to rejoin the company. As he started to walk down the hill, he turned around to look at Sarge and me and said I'm damn proud of both of you, and I'm glad you're both in my company.

As I was walking down the hill, I was thinking to myself. That was probably our pat on the back right after that kick in the ass. We rejoined the company and were prepared to move out to whatever was next.

Chapter X

FOLLOWING A COWARD

We were about a week in our patrols since engaging the sniper and all the firing from the bunker on the hill. Up till now, it has been relatively calm. We only have been bothered by the continuing nuisance of the jungle. One morning while I was enjoying my C-ration and breakfast. I heard a chopper approaching our area. We weren't alerted of choppers coming in, so this is a total surprise.

I could see a chopper getting close by and a clearing next to us. I could observe three soldiers jumping out of the chopper and one soldier getting aboard simultaneously. Then immediately, the chopper was up and away. I couldn't wait to get the news of this transaction.

A few hours later, we got the latest gossip of new replacements. We were informed that after a briefing with the Lieutenant, we would all get a chance to get acquainted. Shortly after lunch, the Lieutenant brought over to our squad another very young-looking Sergeant and told us that this would be our new squad leader and that we all would have a chance to get better acquainted later.

Somebody hollered; what happened to our other Sarge? The quick answer was that he was transferred to another company. I couldn't help thinking that the transfer might have something to do with our two men charging up the hill a week earlier. I will never know the answer, but it would be my good guess.

I was getting bad vibes from the Sergeant during the introduction just by his appearance. His fatigues were clean, and his boots weren't shined, but they weren't dirty either. His black hair was slicked back and almost combed. He looked like he just left basic training. While I was standing there looking at him, all I could think about was to roll around in the dirt for about half an hour.

The time to prove himself would finally come five days later when we were tramping along this somewhat path along a hillside, trying to work our way to the top to dig in for the night. Suddenly, the shit hit the fan, and bullets flew everywhere, ripping twigs and branches around us. The order came quick and loud to get the hell off the path.

We followed the rest of the patrol and crawled to the left and down a ridge that supplied temporary cover. It seemed apparent to us immediately that we were caught in an ambush. The cries for a medic were coming from several different areas as we were all busy firing into the bushes where the ambush was coming from. I could hear our M-60 machine gunner firing as rapidly as he could. A few minutes later, I heard our radioman giving our position and demanding support.

The medic was kept busy crawling to various positions, giving first aid to the wounded. We haven't heard about any casualties at this point, but I was sure we'd have a few. At the rate we were firing our weapons, I wondered how much longer we could be firing at this rate before running out of ammo. That was beginning to worry me, besides the idea of getting hit. For the first time in my life, I was starting to feel like a fish in a barrel.

It was about two hours into this fierce battle of exchanging gunfire as we were taking in more casualties. It also was about the same time that we called in for support. We knew the area was extremely thick with jungle-like terrain, and our engagement was too close for artillery backup. We didn't know for sure what help, if any, was coming to our aid. The question now was, how much longer could we hold on?

It seemed like the last few hours our entire squad had crawled down to what seemed like a ravine or some gully. We all were returning gunfire while still trying to reserve our ammunition without jeopardizing any of our squad members.

I looked around to find my new Sergeant, and what I saw, I couldn't believe my eyes. I saw this Sarge lying on his back in the gully with his rifle across his chest, with his leg standing straight up in the air. He was purposely exposing his leg to sure gunfire.

I thought this son of a gun was looking for an easy way out of this war and a sure pass to go home. At that point, I was so damn mad I could have crawled over and shot him, but not in the leg. I also noticed that we were almost four hours into this battle, and there was no way we could evacuate our wounded.

I was taking count of my ammo in between firing my ass off. I was running close to empty with the same feeling in my stomach. I made up my mind that I was going to save one magazine of ammo to battle to the very end.

A short time later, the word came down only to fire if we came face to face with the enemy. Reinforcements were dropped into the area on all sides of the enemy and were engaging in gunfire with them. We were instructed to stay low and keep alert. I looked over to see my Sarge, who by now was lying in his regular position with his weapon in his arms.

Within minutes we heard gunfire so loud that you would have thought it was the 4th of July. Then occasionally, you could see a few enemies popping out of the brush while trying to escape our reinforcements. These individuals trying to flee instantly became easy targets as none had their hands up in the air to surrender.

This intense firing lasted for almost an hour, and I started to get the feeling that I was being reborn. Shortly we heard voices hollering to hold our fire as we began to see our troops emerging from the brush. I had to control myself from running over and shaking their hands. They soon made a human path for us to get off the hillside and make it to the waiting choppers.

The wounded and dead were evacuated first, and we were all lining up to go down this path behind. I told my Sarge what I saw; I mentioned that he intentionally left his leg exposed for the longest time. I told him I had lost all respect for him and wouldn't even follow him into the bathroom. In return, he never said a word to me and just walked away like it never happened.

As the days passed, I also informed him that if he gave me any shit about the incident, I would go to the Lieutenant and tell him exactly what I saw. He seemed content with the situation for now, and nothing more was said. Only a short time later, he got punctured in the leg with a pungi stick and eventually had to be evacuated. I never saw him after that, and I always wondered, even to this day, if that was also self-inflicted.

Learning to break my weapon down for general cleaning during leadership training.

Chapter XI

CHRISTMAS EVE

I n four days, we would be approaching yet another holiday, and that would be Christmas. It wasn't looking like Christmas around here, and you would never guess it was that time of year. We have spent 90% of our time in Vietnam walking, tramping, and stumbling through jungles, hills, mountains, swamps, and even rice paddies. We never came across anything that resembled a Christmas tree.

While everyone was probably looking for a package or letter from loved ones back home, I was no exception, as I thought the best gift of all was to stay alive during the holidays. There was supposed to be a ceasefire agreement between the two governments, but we knew you could not trust the North Vietnamese. The ceasefire was to last a week from Christmas through the New Year, but most of us didn't believe a word of it. Time will tell in a few short days.

It was late afternoon, during the pouring rain while splashing around in the jungle, when we heard rumors of our whereabouts during the Christmas holiday. It seemed there had been several bombings in the last few weeks along Highway I, attempting to slow down our supply trucks. This route was used constantly, and getting supplies to our troops was crucial.

We heard that our company had been chosen to protect a few of the bridges on this road. This road ran for hundreds of miles and had several bridges along its route, so we could be placed anywhere. The last two episodes on this road weren't too pleasant. While digging our foxholes for the night, we got the official news that the rumors about Highway I were true. I would be getting all the details in the morning after breakfast.

The Lieutenant was standing before us the following morning, explaining our mission. He told us that we were going to guard these bridges for a total of two days. These days would be Christmas Eve day and night and Christmas Day. I couldn't think of a worse Christmas present as I still had a bad feeling about that Highway.

Word had it that the Vietcong planned to blow up as many bridges as possible during the holidays and the so-called ceasefire. He also explained that each squad in the company would be assigned a bridge to protect, which meant our company was temporarily split up.

The mission started sounding a little dangerous with the company being separated. It was also explained that if any of the bridges came under attack, choppers were close by to come to our support. Somehow that news didn't give me much comfort.

We were instructed that the choppers would pick us up in the morning. That will be Christmas Eve day, to take us to our bridges. When the choppers arrived that morning, it only took about twenty minutes to reach our destination.

Each squad was dropped off at a different bridge along the Highway. The bridges were several miles apart from each other. We immediately started inspecting our bridge and its surroundings. The total bridge length was approximately two hundred feet and about fifty feet wide.

A small stream of water ran under the bridge about twelve feet wide and approximately three feet deep. The ditches under the bridge consist of large stones with smaller pebbles. Digging our foxholes with this terrain would be challenging, so we were informed that we would be placed under the bridge in various strategic positions.

The ultimate plan was that two men would walk the bridge at the same time, starting from different ends of the bridge and passing each other in the middle. The walking time on the bridge was only two hours long, and when we got relieved, you were allowed to sleep under the bridge the best you could.

It was my luck I was chosen with another soldier to walk the bridge from 11:00 PM Christmas Eve until 1:00 AM Christmas morning. I couldn't help thinking that I was heading up to the bridge to take my shift, and these hours were supposed to be the most dangerous time of the night.

I felt eerie as my partner, and I started walking the bridge from opposite ends. I felt like a duck in a shooting gallery as we were easy targets for any sniper. While walking and observing the surroundings, I couldn't help letting my mind drift back home to family and loved ones.

I know that it being Christmas Eve, they were warm, safe, and probably tucked in for the night, waiting for Christmas morning. My Christmas wish at the time was to live to another Christmas, to rejoin the same loved ones I left behind a short time ago.

We were about halfway through our shift, and as my partner and I passed each other on the bridge, I thought I heard a faint sound of music. At that moment, I motioned to my partner to join me in the middle of the bridge. When we were together on the bridge, I explained that I thought music was coming from somewhere. Just then, he pulled a small transistor radio out of his pocket.

This was against all rules and regulations, and he asked me not to tell anyone. I promised I wouldn't and asked him to turn it on and keep it low for just a few minutes. He agreed, and a song came on that just blew my mind.

It was Connie Francis singing Silent Night. I instantly grabbed his arm gently and asked him to stay with me until the song was over, and he agreed. About halfway through the song, I could feel my eyes fill up with water, and soon, a few tears came trickling down my cheeks.

After the song ended, my partner looked at me and asked if I was alright. I whispered back that everything was fine while wiping the tears away and suggested we start walking our post on the bridge again.

Little did I know then that this song would haunt me every Christmas Eve or anytime I heard it during the season for the rest of my life. The song or that time of year would always place me back on that bridge. We finished the shift without mishaps and returned under the bridge to finish the night. I couldn't sleep the entire night as one-hundred different thoughts were racing around.

During the day, as we were moving to our destination, rumors were flying that two bridges had been attacked. We heard there were wounded, and casualties on both sides, but the Vietcong were unsuccessful in blowing up the bridges.

Once again, I thanked the Good Lord for letting me live through this Christmas holiday, and for just a moment, I even thought I might live to see another Christmas.

Chapter XII

A Tragic Accident

Our next destination and environment were similar to other patrols in the past several months. After a few days into the patrol, it was explained to us that we would soon be approaching a small village.

We were also told that the villagers were hiding Vietcong soldiers amongst its people. If this were true, it would be almost impossible to tell them apart without a gun in their hand. They all wore black-type pajamas with or without a shirt and straw-like hats.

While approaching a clearing, we could observe a dozen or so grass huts with women and children walking around. We surrounded the village the best we could and started walking toward the huts. Once we were directly in front of the huts, the Sergeant ordered the women to open the doors of all the huts. This precaution was taken because of other mishaps in previous raids.

In some village raids, one soldier would kick in the door of a hut and set off an explosion, killing or wounding everyone nearby. In some cases, they would hang very poisonous snakes in the doorways. When bitten by one of these reptiles, you need medical attention immediately.

After the women had all the doors open in this particular raid, we entered and searched around very thoroughly. During the entire search, not one weapon was found. Most of all, we didn't find a single male hiding anywhere.

The village women told us that all the men were hunting in the jungle. They wouldn't tell us what they were hunting for. Before leaving the village, we conducted a thorough search of the grounds. Shortly we found a cover and, when lifted, exposed a tunnel.

The Sergeant standing over the tunnel was hollering commands for everyone hiding below to come out with their hands up. After several minutes and numerous commands, there was still no activity in the tunnel. The Sergeant had ordered one of our men to throw a flare into the tunnel. He pulled the pin and sent the flare flying into the tunnel. Immediately we could hear coughing and choking, and within seconds people started crawling out of the tunnel with their hands in the air.

The first two men must have taken the flare head-on as their faces were completely purple. Within a few moments, six men came from the tunnel and stated that there was nobody else in the tunnel.

After a few minutes, the Sergeant pulled the grenade from his belt, pulling the pin and letting it fly into the tunnel. The ground rumbled and shook as smoke came bellowing from the tunnel entrance. After a short search, the back to the tunnel was never found, but we thought it was some distance away out in the jungle.

We secured the prisoners' hands behind them and placed them in the middle of the village to await the choppers to take them away, which took about two hours. We were finally heading out to reach our next destination, and I heard we also were running behind schedule. By the time we reached our objective, it was already getting dusk.

The order came down for everyone to dig their foxholes and set up their flares around the perimeter before dark. Once all that was done, we could sit in our foxholes and try to enjoy our evening meal. It was past midnight; all was quiet when several of our perimeter flares suddenly started going off.

Immediately we could hear rapid gunfire being exchanged from some of our foxholes. Within minutes, more flares went off, and more firing followed. The noise was becoming deafening from all the gunfire, as our foxhole was also engaging by now.

At times, the gunfire was coming so rapidly that it made me believe we were surrounded. We could hear voices from our leaders, but because of all the noise, we couldn't fully understand what they were saying. The fact that it was total darkness made it more confusing and disorientated.

As you were constantly firing your weapon out in front of you, you had to keep looking at both sides and even behind you, as you weren't sure they hadn't penetrated our perimeter. At times you couldn't hear firing from some of the neighboring foxholes, making you think they were possibly getting hit by gunfire or running out of ammo; either situation wasn't good.

I could estimate that we had been exchanging gunfire for almost two hours without signs of easing up anytime soon. Empty ammo magazines were starting to clutter up our foxhole; the thought of totally running out was constantly in my mind. About thirty minutes later, the incoming fire started easing up just a little.

We can now hear and understand the orders that are leaders were shouting. One of these orders was for everyone to check the foxholes on both sides of them for casualties or wounded. A short time passed, and it seemed the enemy gunfire had come to a halt. We were firing sporadically to let them know we would fight until the last man was standing.

About ten minutes later, leaders gave the order to halt our fire. The silence was overwhelming and almost frightening. The order also came to stay in our foxhole and to remain quiet and alert until the light of dawn.

My adrenaline was still racing, and I was shocked at what happened. I was also afraid of what we would discover when daylight finally came. It did remain peaceful the rest of the night.

At the light of dawn, we were informed that medics would be jumping around foxhole to foxhole checking for casualties. We were also ordered to halt all firing while he was completing his rounds. When the medic was finished, we were told to check around our foxholes and pick up flares that hadn't been tripped during the night.

While cleaning up our areas, our leaders attended to more important details like handling the wounded and dead. I'm sure they had their hands full trying to figure out all that happened during the night.

We were finally allowed to gather our thoughts, relax, and have our breakfast while a few of our leaders were checking the area. We also were told that we lost one of our Lieutenants last night during the battle. We all remembered him as a good man and great Lieutenant who truly cared about his men. He will surely be missed.

The choppers would be arriving soon to take out all the wounded and dead. I don't remember the total number of casualties and wounded, but we were told that the enemy was ten times worse. My squad was chosen to help carry the wounded and dead to all the choppers. It's hard to explain the sinking feeling you had in your stomach while performing this final task for all these brave and honorable young men. When everyone was evacuated, we were asked to gather for information as our captain would talk to us.

The captain was standing before us with a very stern but sad expression. He would state the conditions and facts of what just happened during the night. He was very respectful of the wounded and dead as we all bowed our heads in prayer. As he praised us, he also mentioned that we were responsible for a tragic accident.

It seems that our Lieutenant was killed by one of our own men during the night as he was checking and crawling from foxhole to foxhole. We were told that he probably got disorientated due to all the firing and the darkness and crawled out in front of one of the foxholes.

I'm sure I was not the only one getting a sickness feeling in my stomach and thoughts of remorse and sorrow. The captain finished by saying that accidents happen, and his family will only be notified that he was killed in battle defending his country. With all that in mind and behind us, we were told to be more careful in the future and be ready to move out within the hour.

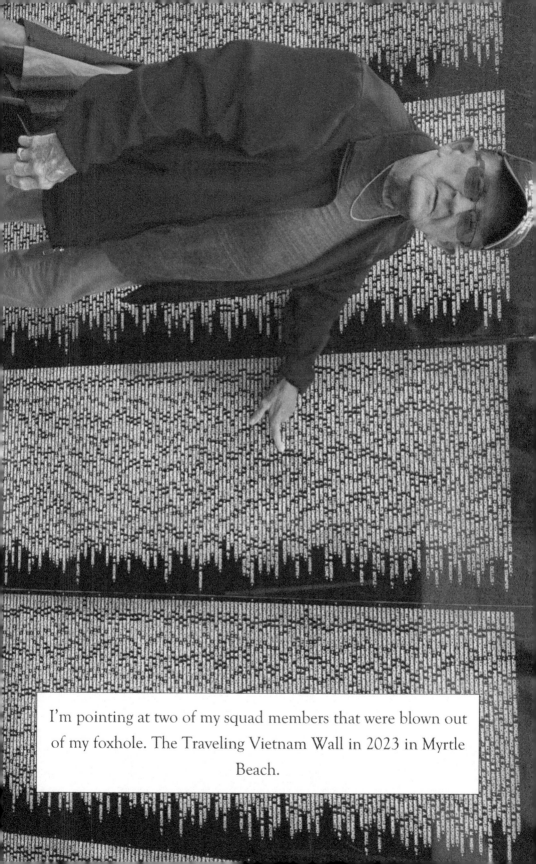

I'm pointing at two of my squad members that were blown out of my foxhole. The Traveling Vietnam Wall in 2023 in Myrtle Beach.

Chapter XIII

HELPING OTHERS

From time to time, choppers would fly into our area at the spur of the moment, and within minutes, we would be off to assist other fellow soldiers. We frequently would get our orders just seconds before jumping into the choppers.

At certain times we would fly into an area to assist and support, and within a few hours, we could be out of there without losing a single person. Other times we would be in a support situation and possibly be there for a day or two. This is the type of situation that I'm going to explain next.

It was early in the morning, just after we had finished our breakfast, that we got the order to get ready to move out, as the choppers would be here in about ten minutes. We also were told that we were going to assist a company that the Vietcong pinned down in a valley that was just a short distance from us. The choppers soon arrived, and we were off once again.

At least you know when you're flying into a situation like this that you will encounter immediate action, and there wouldn't be any big surprises. When the choppers dropped us off, we were told to make some perimeter outside the valley. We could hear the tremendous firepower going on all around us. Once the perimeter was formed, our next orders were to start digging our foxholes as we would be here for a while.

The word finally came down that the enemy surrounded the company we were here to support. We were also informed that we were sending a squad out to try and give them an escape route back to our perimeter.

Another squad was sent down into the valley toward all the firepower. This is one time for sure that I was happy that my squad wasn't picked for either assignment. Both squads were gone for about thirty minutes, and the firing seemed more intense.

Word came quickly that one of our squads came under heavy gunfire and was making their way back to our perimeter to have two of their men to be evacuated. We were told not to fire until the entire squad safely returned to our perimeter. The medivac choppers were already called for as we learned that one soldier was wounded in the stomach, and the other took injuries to his shoulder. We also heard that the other company had suffered several casualties and wounded. They also needed help getting their men evacuated.

Our captain at that time gave the order to call in rocket-firing choppers and machine gun choppers for further and needed support. It wasn't long before the sky above us was filled with rocket ship choppers and machine gunners blowing up the surrounding area. Their mission was to remove the enemy and create a safe pathway to allow the company to get its casualties and wounded back inside our perimeter.

This barrage of machine gun fire and the rocket ship choppers lasted over thirty minutes. As soon as all the choppers left the area, we saw several medevac choppers coming in for a landing. Within twenty minutes, many wounded were being evacuated to the closest hospital. More wounded and casualties had to be evacuated, so we waited for more choppers to arrive.

The sound of gunfire was down to a trickle now and then. With our help and support, our other squad entered the valley river bed from the opposite side. Our squad leader told us to move out and join the other squad along the riverbed. Once we approached the riverbed, we started getting enemy fire from the other side of the river basin.

We had our grenade launcher fire several rounds into the bushy area across the basin, along with our machine gunner firing repeatedly and the same area. Finally, with all the enemy firing ceased, our leader told us to move out and advance further up the river bed to join the other company. All along the way, we came across several Vietcong dead bodies. We couldn't help but notice that many of these bodies looked like young boys.

Up around the riverbed, we started to meet up with some of the men from the other company. We informed them that we were there to assist them with their wounded and casualties to get back to our perimeter.

Man-made structures were used to carry our casualties, and we all assisted in helping the wounded. Our other squad had joined us to help with assisting. While working our way back to the perimeter, a few men were appointed to follow us and guard both sides of the river bed. The going was slow because of the wounded, but at least coming back to our premier, we weren't getting any resistance. Finally, we could see daylight from the sun in the clearing, and we knew that our foxholes and the company were just ahead.

Once everyone was behind our perimeter, we returned to our foxholes that we dug earlier to avoid further attacks. We were now waiting for the chopper to arrive to remove the dead. They finally landed in our area. The wounded were moved immediately, while the casualties took longer as their body bags had to be tagged and prepared.

In the meantime, the other company was starting to dig their foxholes before darkness came. It looked like both companies would spend the night in the area. I was sitting in my foxhole thinking that I never took count of all the dead and wounded that had just left. One was one too many, whether it be wounded or casualty.

Our leaders called for heavy artillery support in the surrounding areas for most of the night. As tired as everyone was, nobody got much sleep. Our artillery support seemed a little too close for comfort, which may be another reason we didn't get much sleep. The rest of the night was peaceful except for all the noise of the artillery, which was also like music to my ears.

Sitting in my foxhole during the night, I couldn't help but think what a devastating day we all had. Soon it would be daylight, and I wondered what day it would be tomorrow. I could just hope and pray that it won't be a duplicate of today.

When dawn approached, artillery firing stopped, and everyone was starting to have breakfast. Shortly after eating, the word was that we would send out two more squads to look over the area. My squad was one of the two picks for the patrol, which was moving out in about thirty minutes. My nervous feeling was now turning into knots in my stomach as we were lining up to move out. It looked like I was about the middle of the patrol.

About twenty minutes in, the patrol started coming across several dead bodies and body parts all over the area. We had to check all the bodies to see if they were still breathing and to ensure they weren't playing possum.

Our two squads began to spread out to sweep the entire area extensively. All we found was more of the same thing. We've been out here on our search and destroy mission and haven't encountered any live enemy or received any firing. The knots in my stomach were starting to loosen up, but the nauseous feeling was taking over. I was sure it was from the smell of all these dead bodies. That is a smell that you will never forget.

We had been out searching for almost two hours, and our leader said we were returning to meet up with our companies. That was the best news that I've heard all day. I couldn't wait to return and feel the comfort and safety of being with my company. The bodies and parts we were leaving behind were too many to count, so our leaders just took an estimation, and the figure just blew my mind.

The all-night barrage of artillery had done its job. Our leaders suggested that because of all the bombing from the artillery, the Vietcong that was left had moved out of the area. Once you all were back inside our perimeter. You could hear a big sigh of relief from everyone. The expressions on everyone's faces went from worry to a new look of hope for what the day would bring.

Our leader said we would be flying out soon and ensure everything was in order. The two companies spent the remaining time waiting for the choppers by shaking hands and wishing each other the best of luck. We never really got to know each other personally, but we all knew what we just shared would last us a lifetime.

Chapter XIV

LEECH HILL

No matter where you were in Vietnam, if you were in the jungles, you came across various creepy crawling creatures. Most of them were readily recognized, while others looked almost prehistoric. Two of the most prominent predators and pests were army ants and leeches. Both creatures were waiting to bite you and attach themselves to your skin to start sucking your blood. Vietnam had a variety of leeches, but they all served one purpose: to suck blood from either another animal or a human. Army ants had the same purpose in mind, but they weren't as prevalent or annoying as the leeches.

You would soon learn to live with these two critters as they and many others just became a part of your everyday life. There were only two things that mattered, and that was you were alive today and were trying to stay alive tomorrow.

We never really came across these critters in abundance until the patrol we were starting to undertake. We were approaching a hill nicknamed Leech Hill, and we were about to find out why. We weren't ten minutes into climbing this hill when the sound of leeches echoed down the line.

Orders followed shortly to button up and tie down, which meant securing any possible opening of your clothing to keep these critters from crawling into. First, you tied down and tucked your pants securely into your boots. Then you ensured your shirt was fully buttoned around the neck and tightened fast inside your trousers.

At present, you weren't too worried about the enemy as you had your hands full with the situation of these blood-sucking critters. These leeches we were about to encounter were known as tiger leeches, about an inch and a half in length and very bloodthirsty.

No matter how airtight you thought you had all your clothing, these little blood-sucking critters would find a way to get into your skin. The immediate mission was to climb up and over this hill, looking for the enemy, just like other patrols in the past. The only problem was that this hill was infested with leeches.

These leeches would cling to any foliage on the ground, hang on branches, twigs, or leaves, just waiting for you to brush by so they could latch onto you. On this patrol, each soldier followed each other a little closer than normal so they could brush off any leeches on the backs of the soldier in front of them.

All your clothing consisted of buttons instead of zippers, which gave them easy access to the slightest opening. Once they entered your clothing, it wouldn't be long before you would feel them biting. At this point, I wasn't expecting to come across any Vietcong for a while because they probably knew better about the area's environment.

The only alternative you had once the leeches' started biting was to try and crush them as fast as they were sucking away. If you could not achieve this, the leech would keep sucking blood until it was full and almost bursting. The leech would detach itself and fall away. Whether you crush them, or they fall off on their own, you would still be left with a bite mark that eventually would cause a small infection that would need medical attention.

The most agonizing entry by one of these critters would be in one of your boots or sometimes both. You couldn't hold up the patrol to sit and remove your boot to remove any critters. You would try to crush it near the area you felt the bite and hope for the best. If you don't properly succeed, it could become a little painful. Sometimes you would use the butt end of your rifle to try and crush them in your boot and try not to break your ankle.

We were about two hours tramping through this torturous terrain when we all heard a cry for a medic. This was a mystery because we didn't hear any explosion or gunfire. Just like always, when we heard the cry for a medic, everybody would freeze in place.

While we were all waiting to hear what the hell just happened, the tiger leeches were having a feast on us. Finally, word came down that one of the soldiers from another squad had a serious problem with the leeches.

It seemed that they crawled into his trousers and were causing havoc with his genitals, and everything was starting to swell. The medic told our leader that the soldier had to be evacuated immediately. Our leader, our Captain, had radioed for a chopper to meet us on top of the hill in about two hours.

Knowing we might be out of this Leech-infested area in a few hours was heartwarming. The man-made stretcher was put together to carry the soldier to the top of the hill. The further climb up the hill; it seemed almost like the leeches were becoming less of a nuisance. As we began to reach the top of the hill, we could see sunlight filtering between branches and bushes.

The top of the hill was a lot drier, and leeches were finally nowhere to be found. When we reached the clearing at the top of the hill, the chopper was waiting for the disabled soldier.

While they were getting him aboard the chopper, we were all hollering good luck and best wishes as we were constantly brushing off the remaining leeches on us. About twenty minutes after the chopper left, we finally got some good news that we would spend the night on top of the hill.

I can only think at this point that some much-needed rest was in-store. I also thought I could handle climbing down the hill much better after a little sleep. My only thought was I hoped the climb down the hill would be better than the climb up.

For now, everyone was opening their cans of C-rations to try to enjoy an evening meal before digging their foxholes for the night. After eating, I suddenly remembered what was eating at my feet all day. A few leeches had also worked their way into my boots during the day. Once the boots were removed, I noticed a few dead leeches that left my socks a bloody mess.

I continued to remove my socks and squeeze the blood out of them. I was trying to let them dry when I decided to do a complete body check. I was finding bite marks from my shoulders down to my legs. I started applying rubbing alcohol all over each bite to help with the infection that would follow.

When I was starting to get my clothes back on, I was checking my backpack, and I was amazed that I found a dry pair of socks. After fully dressed, I buried my bloody socks a safe distance away. Now the last chore for the evening was to dig my foxhole, try to relax, and keep watch for the night. The entire night was quiet and peaceful from the enemy and even our predator leeches.

When Morning arrived, we were all trying to enjoy our breakfast when we got some fantastic news. The previous plans had changed. In a few hours, the choppers would arrive to take us to a new unknown location.

Chapter XV

THOUGHTS OF HOME

At different times I would spend a week or two without even firing a single shot or being fired upon. I would just be dealing with all the horrible conditions of the jungle and its critters and creatures. Most of the critters I came across I didn't know or recognize what they were, or even if they were poisonous.

It would be these quiet times that during a break from the patrol or mealtime, I would let my mind wander about happier times at home. By this time, I was sorely missing my family and loved ones and all the activities that revolved around them.

I would think of the simple things I did every day that seemed monumental. I would love to drive my car, whether it would be for shopping or out for a leisure trip. It was all these simple things that you missed after all these months. It wasn't the quiet times that would cause thoughts of the home front. It would be different daily events that I would go through.

I would think of home while taking a piss or a dump and how much I missed sitting on the toilet and the enjoyment of just flushing it. I was genuinely amazed at all the little things that would trigger the thoughts at home, if only for a few seconds.

Almost every single night while I was trying to sleep in that dirty insect-infested foxhole. My mind would travel to those warm and comfortable nights in the clean sheets and blankets in my bed back home.

Even when I was chowing down on a cold can of C-rations, I would remember how easy it was to put a quick meal on the stove and push a button to enjoy a very delicious hot meal in a matter of minutes. Whenever I let my mind wander back home for even a few seconds, I was always aware of my surroundings and never let my guard down for a moment.

When I often took a tiny sip of water from my canteen, trying to conserve my water supply, my thoughts once again would travel back home. I could picture myself at my kitchen sink, letting the water overflow into my glass to quench my thirst.

It didn't take much, whether day or night, to trigger these spontaneous thoughts of home. My hygiene was always utmost on my mind and made me think of what I was missing while not in the comfort of my own home. I've been walking in these jungles for over four months and have yet to enjoy a shower, hot or cold. Many days I would think of the long hot showers back home.

When I'm thinking of a shower back home, I'm also fantasizing about all the accessories that accompany it, like soap, shampoo, deodorant, and, yes, even cologne. I must be totally honest; I don't think a day went by while living in these treacherous jungles that I didn't have a flashback moment of home. It was easy to let your mind slip back during a relaxing time, whether day or night, if only for a few seconds.

I can't tell you how many times I caught myself visualizing just sitting in the comfort and safety of my home with my family or a loved one simply watching TV together. These flashbacks would come often, but they would always be short-lived. They didn't stick around for any time, as you still had a war to continue with. It wouldn't be fair to yourself or your fellow soldiers to let your mind wander from your too long.

Although these constant thoughts of home brought many happy memories and enjoyment of various activities before going to Vietnam, there was also a downside to all these positive and enjoyable moments.

It also meant that what I was now enjoying a thought was only a past tense to what I was going through in the present. It would, sometimes, bring immediate thoughts of depression and self-pity to my current situation. These happy thoughts were almost like a double-edged sword. It could slice you either way.

I often wondered if I was fortunate enough to live and make it through this war and back home if I would have not happy thoughts but flashbacks of all my war experiences. For now, my only thought was there's no place like home.

Chapter XVI

Rappelling from a Helicopter

Our support helicopters often couldn't pick us up or even drop us off in different areas because of the dense environment. This would cause severe difficulties numerous times throughout our maneuvers. It wasn't long before our leaders decided that each platoon needed a rappelling squad, and yes, my squad was the one chosen. This meant practicing jumping out of tall trees for hours at a time for several days under trained instructors. We were given heavy leather rappelling gloves and extra-large hooks, which we always had to carry.

Once it was thought that we were sufficiently trained, my squad was designated to lead all assaults in densely covered areas where our choppers had a problem landing. This new assignment was extremely dangerous and sharply decreased my chances of making it through this war.

Whenever our platoon was called to support another company, my squad was chosen to lead the way. If the enemy fire was too heavy for the choppers to go in for a landing, we would rappel quickly from the choppers and try to scamper to safety.

At times like this, I thought this rappelling squad was more like a suicide squad. Even though I wasn't getting a weekly paycheck, I was almost certain that I wasn't getting any extra pay. Before we would jump out of that chopper and start our descent, the machine gunners would be blaring away on the ground below to try and give us ample cover.

The rappelling ropes were lowered from both sides of the chopper, and with our weapons around our necks, we waited for the command to jump. You had your jumping hook and leather gloves ready to go. The machine guns were so loud you couldn't hear if the enemy was returning fire.

Just before I got the order to jump, I couldn't explain the feeling that came over me except it felt like I was jumping into hell. When the order finally came, you hooked up to the rope and tried to slide to the ground as fast as possible. It only took a few seconds, but it felt much longer.

Once on the ground, you would grab your weapon and start firing away because, by now, the machine gun firing had ceased. Our immediate job was to try and subdue the area to make it safe for the choppers to land, to bring other soldiers in. Between all the machine gun firing and all the firepower from our squad, once we were on the ground, it was usually enough to create a safe and secure environment for others to follow.

During my entire stay in Vietnam, I only had to use my rappelling skills in two locations. Once, it was because the area was so dense the choppers couldn't land. We were sent in to repel down and clear out an area large enough for several choppers to land at one time. This type of rappelling was less nerve-wracking than the other while you were under enemy fire. Enough though, you were still an easy target for snipers hiding in the lower bushes or trees.

In my two descents, we never lost a man while sliding down our ropes, but once we hit the ground was a different situation.

There was only one minor injury that I can remember while rappelling, and that was self-inflicted. Just before we were about to rappel, the soldier in our squad noticed his gloves were missing. He started panicking, and then we got the order to jump.

This was one of the times we were under fire, and the machine guns were firing away. I'm sure when it came to his turn to grab the rope, the only thought I'm sure he had was to get to the ground as quickly as possible. I learned later that he had lost most of his skin on both hands and needed medical attention from our medic. I saw him a short time later, and his hands were heavily bandaged, and he wore a pair of socks to keep them clean. To this very day, I'm unsure if this young soldier ever got evacuated.

I was truly satisfied and almost esthetic that I only had two experiences with rappelling. I often thought my training was like telling a young firefighter he would get a few training days before sending him into a burning building. Maybe it wasn't a fair comparison, but that was exactly how I felt.

Chapter XVII

AGONIES OF THE VIETNAM WAR

Just like in any war, if you were in the infantry, being a so-called ground soldier, you would see a great amount of bloodshed in death. You would also witness a monumental amount of personal misery. The only upside I could see in possibly hope for was to live through all this shit and return home with all the body parts I came with.

It was enough to deal with all the blood and guts on the battleground that would probably last me a lifetime of nightmares. Then you had to be subject to all the deplorable conditions daily. Let us take my average day in the jungles of Vietnam and put aside all the fighting for the next 24 hours.

When you were awake early in the morning, it didn't matter how much sleep you got the previous night, if any at all. While you were crawling out of your dirty filthy, and bug-infested foxhole, you only had one major thought on your mind: please,

Lord, let me live another day. This would only mean that you would be one day closer to getting the hell out of here.

You started the day by trying to brush off all the dirt and any remaining bugs that might be left on you from the night. No matter how much or little sleep you got during the night, you would splash just a little water on your hands to try and wipe the sleep from your eyes.

If you thought you needed a shave, you would dry shave so you wouldn't waste more water than necessary. Water and ammunition were the two most important items to keep you alive. It's precious, as they both were. You treated them like gold.

I also tried to brush my teeth at least twice a day, once in the morning after breakfast and sometime later in the evening. Once again, you would only take a very small mouthful of precious water to rinse the toothpaste from your mouth. I never carried mouthwash because it would be an extra burden. I also thought I wasn't over here to kiss the enemy but only to shoot him.

It didn't take me long to realize that everything had to be rationed, including the hygiene products that I used daily. It wasn't like there was a corner store around the bush to replenish any or all my necessities. This is also true of any of my hair products, which mainly consisted of a basic shampoo to try and clean the dirt and dust from your scalp.

Next, comb or brush your hair, which would depend on the cleanliness of either. If neither were sanitary, you would simply run your fingers through your hair and slap your baseball cap on your head.

Now that you were spic and span, you had breakfast or headed to the bushes to dump. It all depended on which was more important. If breakfast was in order, you simply pulled out your trusty P-38, your little can opener, and started opening your breakfast choice. Most mornings, he didn't have time to heat the cans, or you were out of your little tablets and stirred up. It didn't matter because, by now, the cold and greasy ham and eggs were starting to taste good.

When it was time for your morning dump, you only needed your toilet paper and your little shovel to bury it. Your morning newspaper was out of the question. Now you are ready to meet the day and face whatever the jungle throws at you.

Most days, the jungle became more of an enemy than the Vietcong. It would torture you, challenge you to your limits, and cut, scratch, and bruise you all over your body. It was relentless and ruthless and never showed any mercy, day or night. It also would harbor a huge variety of critters and creatures that were not human-friendly.

If you accidentally encounter these critters, most of them could cause severe pain, possibly evacuation. Bathroom and smoke breaks were put on hold until the platoon would stop for a brief rest or lunch break. We were always told how long the break would be so we could take care of our priorities.

One of my greatest fears was someday, while on patrol, I would come down with diarrhea. I often thought if it ever happened, I would just be shit out of luck. There is no way that they would stop the patrol every half hour to let me take care of my business. In all my days in the jungle, I never remember seeing a Johnnie on the spot.

Whenever lunch break was called, we were also instructed if it would be thirty minutes or at least an hour. This is important as I might have more important things to do besides lunch. Very seldom would I ever remove my boots during the day unless I had a particular problem with my feet. Boot removal and foot attention was usually left to nighttime while sitting in my foxhole. If I use the mealtime break to do anything other than eat my rations, it better be of some kind of major concern.

Our lunchtime was exactly like every other meal after eating. I had to dispose of all my cans of C-rations and all the trash that went with them. Unlike at home, there aren't any garbage cans scattered throughout the jungle, so I had to gather all the trash with my shovel and dig another hole to bury it all.

It seemed like I was always digging a hole for one reason or another. Except some holes were bigger than others, like my foxhole, almost every night. The only good thing about taking a piss, besides the feeling of relief, was I didn't have to dig a hole to bury it.

I learned very quickly how to ration everything in anything. It almost meant using a small amount of anything I would apply to my body or take orally. This particularly would pertain to my water intake. Even while hacking and tramping through jungles in the heat of the day, no matter how thirsty I got, I always made sure to never gulp down my water.

The best thing I learned early on was to take small sips. These would help you avoid getting sick and preserve your water until you can refill your canteens. I also treated my food in the same manner and made sure not to open another can if I wasn't sure of finishing it. I always remember the old saying "waste not" and "want not," which were never more meaningful than here in the jungles of Vietnam.

Although I always wore a watch, it wasn't essential here in the jungle. The only time that had any significance was whether it was day or night. From very early in the morning, I was told when to eat and when to move out on patrol. I was informed when it was time to stop and take a break and when to stop and eat. I couldn't even remember anyone asking me what time of day it was because it didn't matter. I was also told when to stop for the night, and I automatically knew it was time to have my supper and dig your foxhole for the night.

Tomorrow would almost be a replica of today, except the jungle might produce more scratches, cuts, and bruises. There was always a possibility of running into a sniper or two and getting involved in a firefight. For now, I would enjoy the peace and quiet of my foxhole. While sitting in my foxhole before dark was the only time I had for letter writing. When I would finish the letter, I would have to fold it and keep it dry until a chopper arrived with incoming mail to send it out. I wasn't sure about the time frame for the outgoing mail, but I could testify about how slow the income mail was.

For example, my Christmas box of goodies from my parents didn't arrive until the middle of January the following year. It looked like a truck ran over it, and everything in the box had to be thrown in the garbage, except for a few canned goods. I could only think it was the thought that counted. Fighting over in the jungles of Vietnam consisted of far too many troubling sacrifices. Too numerous to even mention in this chapter. I also had to give up a lot, and I'm very fortunate today that one of these sacrifices wasn't my life.

Another view of the Traveling Vietnam Wall
in Myrtle Beach in 2023

Chapter XVIII

BAD AND WORSE DAYS

Every day in Vietnam for me started as a bad day, and as the day progressed, and never got any better. The only good news was I survived the night and was about to face another bad day. After stopping through these treacherous jungles daily, I was beginning to wonder where in the hell am I getting all this energy from. With all your gear on and the temperature reaching at least 100 degrees on average, I would be sweating from head to toe.

At certain times my body would seem to falter, but my brain was always in a survival mode that would pull me through the weaker moments. At least to this point, my brain wasn't getting fried, and I was still thinking with a clear mind. In the following few weeks, we only encountered a few minor skirmishes, which the front of the platoon took care of quickly.

Not long after, I was starting to lose my appetite, and the day's activities were taking a toll more than usual. It even got to a situation where I gave my fellow soldiers a few cans of my C-rations. Until now, C-rations were only traded daily but were never given away until now. A few thought it was weird, but they never questioned it.

Someone eventually alerted the medic about my behavior, and he finally confronted me about how I was feeling. After explaining my symptoms, he gave me some pills and said he would check on me at least twice daily.

Several days later, my appetite had almost completely ceased. I was starting to give away most of my food, and now the medic was serious about my condition. At this point, I was starting to run a little fever. By this time, the medic was concerned that I might be coming down with malaria. In the past few months, two soldiers from our company had to be evacuated with the disease.

My main problem was that I knew I was feeling much weaker as the days went on. The following day, while on patrol, the soldier behind me hollered and asked if I had to shit my pants. Laughing back, I assured him that I didn't. But he seriously told me that I had a huge stain on the seat of my trousers. For the moment, I thought maybe I might have sat in something.

A few hours later, we all were on a short break, and I decided to drop my trousers and check out what the soldier was hollering about. To my surprise, it seemed to be a stain of dried-up blood. The soldier behind me seemed truly worried and told me to go and talk to the medic. I convinced him I could wait until we stopped for the night and talk to the medic in the morning.

Later, when we stopped for the night, I told my friend I would wash and change my trousers. When I completed that task, I couldn't help but wonder what the hell was going on. During the night, while I was on watch, I had plenty of time to contemplate the total situation. I concluded that I would give it another effort tomorrow to try and stay on the patrol.

While I was having breakfast in the morning, the medic came over to me to check on my situation. I failed to tell him about the blood I found in my trousers. I also agreed to keep him informed of any changes during the day. My friend approached me also and wanted to know my progress. I told him that I and the medic talked and would keep him abreast of anything new during the day. He gave me that look like he didn't believe a word I was telling him.

After we started on patrol, I couldn't help thinking no matter what the day would bring; it would be a long one. About two hours into the patrol, I was starting to get a slight cramping feeling in my stomach. Now I was starting to get alarmed with my physical condition. At this time, I wasn't completely sure if I could make it through the day. It wasn't long after that my friend behind me hollered again about his staying on the rear of my trousers.

Before he had time to check, he was hollering for the medic.

The patrol came to a halt as a medic came running. He immediately saw the problem when he approached me and removed my trousers. When this was done, and he observed the situation, I heard him holler to the captain that we needed a chopper for an evacuation promptly.

As I was waiting for the chopper to evacuate me to the field hospital to evaluate my condition, the medic was trying to explain what was happening. He told me that I was bleeding internally, which was a very serious situation. I thought I was in deep trouble from his tone of voice and demeanor. He assured me the chopper would arrive within an hour and for me to gather all my personal belongings along with my weapon.

When the chopper arrived, and they were loading me onto the stretcher, I gave all my fellow soldiers the usual thumbs up. I could hear them holler to get well and hurry back because they would miss me. While lying in the chopper getting ready for takeoff, I thought I would miss them also, but I was in no hurry to return.

We weren't in the air too long before I knew it; we were coming in for a landing. Once on the ground, it reminded me of something from a movie, as four men in white uniforms came running toward the chopper. Within minutes they were carrying me toward a large medical tent.

Immediately I only had one thought: I was about to sleep in a tent tonight and out of the weather. Things were already starting to look up without knowing why they brought me here.

Before entering the tent, I was told I had to leave all my belongings outside in the corridor, including my weapon. They guaranteed that everything would be returned to me upon leaving the field hospital. This would be the first time in Vietnam that I wouldn't be sleeping with my weapon. Even though I was fully dressed, I still had a naked feeling.

Chapter XIX

VIETNAM FIELD HOSPITALS

Once inside the tent, I saw rows of cots serving as beds. I was escorted about halfway down the tent to a cot waiting for me. For a few moments, I was sure that I was the center of attention which, at this time, I didn't need.

Within minutes, a nurse took my temperature and blood pressure. She followed up by instructing a male orderly to help me with my bath. A warm water and soap basin was brought to my bedside, along with clean towels. Also, a clean pair of pajamas was brought to my bedside. Then I was instructed to bathe and put on a clean nightwear set.

They assured me that all my dirty clothes would be disposed of. Somehow that also made me feel cleaner. No matter how sick I felt, I couldn't believe the events in the last few hours. It almost felt like I was out of the war zone, but I knew I was only a few minutes away. Nonetheless, I enjoyed clean clothes, a bed covering overhead, and a safe and secure feeling. It wasn't exactly a five-star accommodation, but it was the best I had since being in Vietnam.

Also, the fact that I was getting the proper medical attention meant the world to me at the time. I was sure no matter what my problem was, the doctors would cure my illness, and I would rejoin my friends back in the jungle within a few weeks.

I was too sick and in constant pain to think about anything except getting better quickly. The pains in my stomach seem to be increasing by the hour. Now all I was thinking about was getting some rest and sleep. Those thoughts were soon delayed as a nurse approached my bed and told me they had to complete a few tests before I ate supper and retired for the night.

The test didn't take long, and both were painless. Next, she insisted that I try to digest some hot liquids, even though I tried to explain to her that I didn't have any appetite. She also informed me that they would put me on a proper diet after all the tests were completed.

When the food finally arrived, I remember just taking a few sips of each bowl before lying back in bed to relax for the night. As far as bathroom privileges, I was restricted to a bedpan. This was still better than digging a hole and burying it.

During the night, I was awakened a few times for medication and a couple more tests, but I didn't mind a damn bit. Several times during the night, I also asked the orderlies the same questions and always got the same answer. I was concerned about my weapon, and they assured me that it was safe and would be returned to me when I left the hospital.

This will be the first night in over six months that my weapon was not next to me while I was sleeping. Previously, over the months, I had to have my weapon touching me throughout the night so I could get any kind of rest or sleep. I could never imagine awakening during the dark of night during a firefight and start searching for my weapon.

No matter how much pain I was in, I had the feeling of safety and comfort, which I was enjoying. My mind would always drift back to my fellow soldiers back in the jungle. A few times during the day, I was almost feeling guilty.

My night nurse explained that I would be put on a liquid diet until they ran several more tests, trying to determine the cause of my illness. She also told me that tests and blood samples would be carried out during the night. A short time later, she returned to hook me up to an IV unit and said they would change it throughout the night.

Although I realized that steady sleep would be impossible, it would be the first time in Vietnam that I would sleep with both eyes closed. Eventually, all the lights were dimmed, just enough to allow all the medical staff to get around the ward during the night.

During the peaceful and quiet hours of the night, my mind was wondering what and the hell they would find wrong with me and how long I would spend in this field hospital.

The next morning, I was awakened for more tests and given my morning liquids. Except for a few nightly interruptions for medication, it was the greatest night's sleep I had in six months. It wasn't long before I realized we had all made a huge mistake. I was feeling sort of wet in the seat of my pajamas, and once I removed them, to my surprise, and the orderly, the bottom was smeared with fresh blood.

Maybe because of all the tests and excitement of the night's confusion, we all forgot why I was brought here. The main reason I was evacuated from the jungle was loss of appetite, stomach cramps, and bleeding from my rectum. Somehow, we all forgot to put protection in the bottom of my pajamas to catch the blood flow. I'm sure this mishap wouldn't occur again.

After cleaning up and receiving a clean pair of pajamas, I was also given a cloth-like pad to put in the seat of them. I was told to check regularly during the day and night and change the pad when necessary. The nurse came to my bedside shortly after breakfast with a few cups. She explained that one was for a urine sample and the other was for a stool deposit. After providing both samples, I was just lying on the bed, trying to relax and contemplate.

It was now in early May of 1966, and I've already survived six months in the jungles of Vietnam. I had high hopes that I could live through the remaining months between my hospital stay and being sent back to the jungles.

Each day in the hospital meant one less day of getting shot or blown away back in the jungles. I was enjoying my first day and night in the hospital. During the second day, the pains and cramps in my stomach were starting to be unbearable. I remember spending most of the day popping pain pills and lying in a fetal position. I was only taking in liquids while constantly being hooked to an IV bottle.

I occasionally observed new patients coming into the hospital tent during the night or day. Never having the opportunity to talk to them, I was always wondering what their problem was. At this point, I wasn't even sure what the hell was wrong with me. All I could hope for at this time was whatever they found out about my problem, it wouldn't be terminal.

The very next day, my doctor explained to me exactly what the cause of my problem was. He explained that they found two types of parasites inside my body. He went on to say that one of the parasites was a flesh-eating type. At the same time, the other one was just making me sick as hell. He also told me I would only be with them for a few more days. He said they would keep me as comfortable as possible before being shipped out by a chopper to a more equipped hospital to deal with my problem.

Instantly, I sat up on my bed to look the doctor in the eyes. I politely told him, 'Sir,' I absolutely refuse to get on that chopper without my backpack and rifle. He guaranteed me that I would have both just before entering the chopper. I told the doctor that as sick as I was, somehow, that made me feel better.

Two days later and early in the morning, the nurse came to my bed and told me that the chopper was here to take me to another local field hospital. I was also informed to prepare for departure because the stretcher would be here soon.

The nurse told me the IV bottle was staying hooked up to me until I arrived at the new hospital. Before I had a chance to ask, she also stated that my backpack and weapon would be put on the chopper. I just looked up at her and gave her a very satisfactory smile. While they were carrying me out of the tent, all the other patients were waving and hollering best wishes to me. I was waving back and wishing all of them the same.

Chapter XX

A LARGER-THAN-LIFE HOSPITAL IN VIETNAM

While I was flying to another field hospital in Vietnam, I was beginning to worry about how serious the condition that I was in. The flight was relatively short, and we started to land. When they were carrying me on the stretcher, the new hospital looked like a structure instead of a tent. Already things were starting to look better, and once inside the hospital, I no longer thought I was in Vietnam.

As they carried me to my bed, I saw signs of a hospital I hadn't seen in years. It was brightly lit up and seemed medically clean. I soon noticed that the building had running water which meant they could have flushing toilets.

One of the orderlies approached me, tried to make me feel welcome, and said the nurse would be with me in a few minutes. Once the nurse arrived at my bedside, she immediately started to hook up a fresh IV bottle. She told me that after she reviewed all my paperwork, she would get back to me. She also informed me that the staff would handle all my needs.

My stomach felt like it had a lead ball inside it, and all I wanted for the moment was to lie down and rest. The structure even seemed to have air conditioning because the hospital room was very comfortable.

After a short rest, the nurse reappeared and gave me new information about my hospital stay. She let me know that they would be running numerous tests along with some X-rays and blood work. I stayed on my liquid diet with the IV solutions and was restricted to total bed rest. It also meant that I only had bedpan duties and wouldn't get a chance to check out the toilets.

At least by now, with all the tests and medications, they seem to have my rectal bleeding mostly under control. Most of the blood is only showing up in my stool. I had some concerning questions for him and was hoping for just a little good news for a change. He was honest with me and said I had a serious condition that immediately needed medical attention. He also stated that he wasn't sure if they had all the facilities necessary for my recovery. They said they would know better in a few days, and he would let me know. I thanked him for his honesty.

I also wanted to know if my illness was life-threatening, and he assured me it was not. The next question I asked him was when I could return to my outfit in the jungle. He wouldn't answer that; he said, let's worry about getting well first.

The nurse told me that they would conduct several tests in the next few days and continue my pain medicine for my stomach cramps. When I first entered the field hospital, my weight was

182 pounds. I knew then I had lost several pounds from the previous weeks of not eating. I was afraid to think how much weight I would lose on this liquid diet.

I will not detail the numerous tests they put me through but only say that many of these were extremely uncomfortable. On my fourth day at this hospital, I observed an orderly filling a metal tube full of ice. I asked what was going on, and it was very surprising, as he told me they were preparing an ice bath for a malaria patient, and that was a way to get their body temperature down. Anyway, it made me cold just thinking about it.

On the fifth day in the hospital, my doctor came to my bedside with new information. He said that the two parasites in my body were diagnosed as amebiasis and giardiasis. He also stated they both could be cured, but it would take time and certain treatments that weren't available at this hospital.

From his conversation, it sounded like the parasites had already caused some damage to my digestive tract and stomach. This was causing blood in my stool, cramps, stomach pains, and feverish conditions. The latest news from the doctor was that the parasites had already caused an infection within my body, which needed immediate attention.

I was told by the medical staff they couldn't give me any food in my system until the infection condition was cured. Later, the doctor approached my bedside with some updated news. He informed me that they were flying me to another hospital in the

Philippines tomorrow afternoon. He also stated that he would see me in the morning after breakfast with all the details.

Now I was worried about the seriousness of my illness and getting a little tired of playing musical hospitals. This would amount to three hospitals in about six weeks. I was questioning if the medical staff had been honest with me about my condition. I was hoping to get more answers in the morning before my departure.

I was just as worried about my physical being and about returning to the jungle. I couldn't believe that I would be leaving Vietnam, whether it was temporary or permanent. In either situation, I thought about all my friends I was leaving behind.

Finally, morning arrived, and the nurse was the first to my bedside. She gathered all my medications and advised me on what I could expect. She informed me that it would be a long flight and wanted me to be aware of all the medicine. She told me the doctor would be around shortly and fill me in on all the fine details. She let me know if I had any questions; please save them and ask the doctor when he comes around.

It wasn't long before the doctor arrived at my bedside to give me all the details of my next hospital move. He started by telling me that my weapon and ammo had to remain in Vietnam. He said all my personal belongings, along with my backpack, could go along with me. I was to be given enough medicine to last the flight, and I would be hooked up to an IV bottle while I was flying. He also informed me that I had severe intestinal infections that needed serious attention.

The main question I asked the doctor was, what were my chances of returning to the Vietnam War? The answer was that my health and well-being were the most important matter at hand, and my medical team would answer that question once I left here. Right now, the hospital in the Philippines is the next step on the road to your recovery.

Chapter XXI

THE PHILIPPINES

All my medicines and personal belongings were gathered as I was notified that the plane arrived to take me to the Philippines. I was anxious, along with being worried about what this new adventure was going to develop. Anticipation, with a little frustration, were some of my feelings before take-off.

Finally, the orderlies arrived to roll me to my next destination while at the same time trying to assure me that everything was going to be fine. Maybe all the medication was working overtime because I practically slept during the entire flight. The next thing I remember was they were escorting me from the plane and saying welcome to the Philippines.

As they were rolling me to my vehicle, I was constantly looking around to my new surroundings. I was amazed to see numerous brick buildings with several-story-high glass windows. It looked like I finally reached civilization. I thought it was a damn shame to be too sick to enjoy the experience. No matter what, I intended to make the best of being out of a war-torn country.

As we entered the hospital, they were rolling me down a long, huge hallway while I tried to observe as much as possible. When we entered my hospital ward, I immediately saw numerous beds with patients in them.

Besides all the modern appliances and instruments, the most astounding thing I saw that almost blew my mind was the televisions on the walls. It was only a short time before my nurse instructed me on what to expect during my stay here. She explained that I would still be on a liquid diet and be on IV constantly. I would continue to have only bedpan privileges.

I had to ask her when I could expect to have the luxury of having complete and total bathroom opportunities. The answer was when I was free of all my parasites because they didn't want them ending up in their water system. My next question was, could I at least visit the facility to look around? She responded only under supervision. Another question I had was about the T.V. She answered that there was one T.V. for every two beds and that I had to share with the patient next to me. I asked a lot of other questions, and she took the time to answer every one of them.

When all the questions were finished, she continued to say that I would only be here for a short stay and that I would be going to another hospital. She wasn't sure of my next destination but assured me she would let me know in a few days. She also informed me that they would conduct a barrage of tests on me during my visit here.

By this time, I was starting to feel like a guinea pig. Previously, I'd been poked, punctured, probed, and other tests performed on me that I don't want to talk about. I just said to myself, oh, what the hell, this was sure a lot better than being in the jungle of Vietnam.

Shortly after, an assistant came around to start the battery of tests, including blood samples and checking all my vital signs. She also forewarned me of the tests they had scheduled for the rest of the day.

The following day, one orderly showed up at my bedside with a wheelchair, looking slightly bewildered. He said that he was there to show me around in the restroom. He also let me know that using the facility was off-limits to me. I said I know; I was aware of that and just wanted to look around.

He couldn't help himself as he gave out a little chuckle. Smiling, he said. Let me get this straight; I will push you to the bathroom so you can look around. I assured him he was correct, and I told him about my Vietnam experience up until now.

He immediately stopped smiling and ordered me to get out of bed and prepare for my grand bathroom tour. We were both trying to be serious; this would be a hilarious moment at any other time and circumstances. While viewing the facility, we were also trying to keep our composure. Then I jokingly said yep, it's just as I remembered it. Once again, he smiled as he returned me to my bed. Once we met our destination on this wheelchair tour, he turned around and said this is one experience that I'll never forget.

Yes, it was. I returned to my bed and looked the orderly square in the eyes. I said, Sir, I have many experiences I'll never forget. He answered I'm sure you have. As he walked away, he turned around and gave me a salute, which I quickly returned.

Later during the day, while watching T.V., I caught myself laughing out loud during the program bonanza; it seemed everyone on the ponderosa was speaking in a foreign language. As sick as I was, I thought to myself that this was the first time I could remember that I was really enjoying myself.

I couldn't help thinking that there might be light at the end of the tunnel after seven months of misery and mayhem. My main concern was that I constantly lost weight and felt much weaker by the day. My doctor approached me after breakfast the next morning with more puzzling news. He told me they would experiment with a few new advanced tests on me today before shipping me out to Japan tomorrow.

With that news, you could imagine the number of questions I had for him. The first was exactly what kind of test, and the second was where in the hell in Japan? He answered my first question in medical terms, which I didn't understand. The second was. Yokohama, Japan. Both answers were confusing to me. All I knew for certain was that tomorrow I was flying out again, and one more time, it wouldn't be back in the jungles of Vietnam.

Chapter XXII

YOKOHAMA, JAPAN

I was told again that the flight to Japan would be long and they would keep me as comfortable as possible. I don't know what medicine they gave me just before takeoff, but it made me sleep almost the entire flight.

Once we landed, I was transported to a hospital about thirty minutes from the airport. When I arrived in my ward, my nurse awaited me. She had some basic information on my medical situation. She told me I would only be at this hospital for a few days. She said they wouldn't perform any new tests on me while I was there. She also told me they would be continuing my IV and liquid diet. I'd also be restricted to my bed. She explained they were waiting for a bed to open at the other hospital. I would be spending my entire time there while staying in Japan.

This permanent hospital was about an hour away and in Yokohama. At this hospital, I was told that they would continue all my treatments and run more advanced procedures in my total care. Two days later, I was heading to this very hospital.

Upon my arrival, I was immediately escorted to my unit in the hospital. I had already heard many good things about this hospital from the previous one. I already felt like I was in good hands.

After they got me settled in, my nurse appeared to get acquainted and explain my daily agenda. She told me my condition wasn't life-threatening, but I also might be here for a while. She shared that they had all the facilities and laboratories to treat my illness. She said it was too early to tell me if I would be returned to the front lines once my treatments were finished.

She was about to start my IV solution when she looked at my arms and said they were beginning to look like pink cushions with black and blue marks. She explained that she would use one of my legs and give my arms a break and time to heal.

I thanked her, and at that point, I knew I was in good hands. I had a lot on my mind, but my nurse and aide seemed very professional and sympathetic. Your nurse had two duties. She had to perform on me immediately. One was starting the IV, and the other was getting a blood sample. She explained that she would put the IV in my less wounded arm and take the blood specimen from my leg.

While she was drawing the blood sample from my leg, she was shocked about the condition my feet were in. She immediately wanted to know how long my feet were looking like that. I answered everybody saying. My feet were even worse than that long before they evacuated me. During all my hospital stays, I thought they were improving.

The nurse insisted that this would be another problem that needed serious attention. She let me know that she was going to relay this situation to the doctor. Another concern she had was my weight loss, and she was also going to bring that to my doctor's attention.

Up until now, I hadn't met the doctor that was being assigned to me. I was sure he would either be around later during the day or first thing in the morning. The next morning after breakfast, my new doctor was standing by my bedside, enlightening me as to what to expect during my stay there at the hospital. He told me he would oversee my recovery while I was in Japan. He also said he was very concerned about my weight loss rate. He stated that they were going to monitor my weight daily and try to keep it under control.

When I first entered the hospital in Vietnam, I was 182 lbs, and yesterday, they weighed me at 153 lbs. Besides the weight loss and stomach cramps, I felt tired and weak. With my condition, I couldn't write long letters. Still, I always sent postcards from each hospital to family and loved ones, letting them know about my progress.

I calculated my hospital stays up until now, being over three months, meaning that I was losing about ten pounds per month. This also started to worry me just a little. I had a whole list of priorities to be concerned about before my weight loss. They consisted of getting rid of all my parasites, cramps, fever, infections, and my forever and constant sickening feeling.

After all, if those are cured, I could regain my appetite and gain some precious weight. Every day seemed the same routine for the following few weeks, except for some new tests the doctor would run. They also were changing and adding to my medications every few days.

I eventually noticed that I wasn't always lying in a fetal position, meaning the cramps had to be subsided. This was the first positive sign I'd seen in months. In the next few days, I felt like conversing with some of the patients in my ward. Until now, the other patients knew of my circumstances and decided not to bother me while in that condition. Once I opened up to them, they responded by letting me know their feelings.

In the next week or so, I was getting acquainted with my fellow patients. I was hearing stories along with telling some of my own. I was starting to feel better or in a better frame of mind. Even at certain times, I thought I might survive this whole ordeal.

The one thing indifferent between the way I was starting to feel and what my doctors were telling me was confusing. I couldn't wait to start feeling better, along with my medical advisers telling me the same thing.

In Yokohama Hospital in Japan before flying back to the U.S. in 1966.

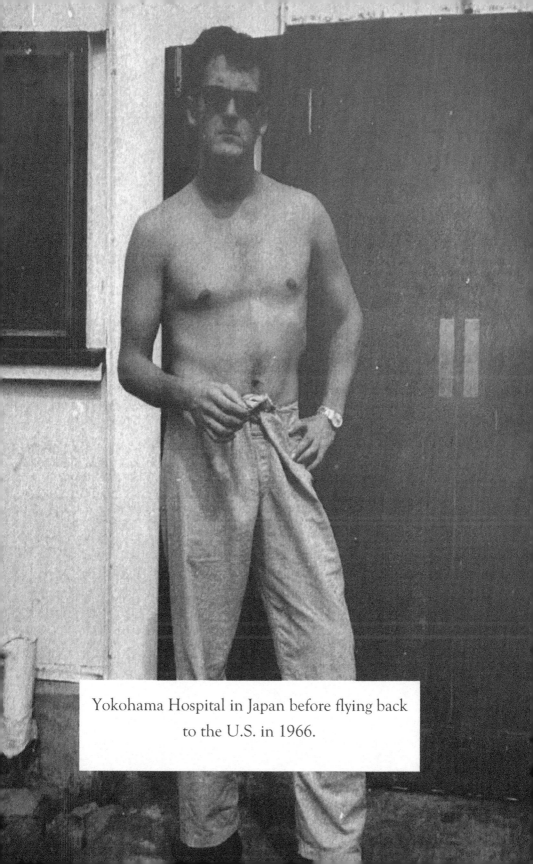

Yokohama Hospital in Japan before flying back to the U.S. in 1966.

Chapter XXIII

THE HAPPIEST DAY OF MY LIFE

Now that I was corresponding with my fellow patients, even though it was on a limited basis, it made the days much more bearable. Though I was still restricted to my bed with my IV and bedpan, my fellow patients would gather around my bedside to engage in friendly conversation. I couldn't help but think all this had to be good therapy.

During the last week, I had lost another 5 lbs., and I was told that the doctor and nurse were coming in the morning to discuss the matter with me. The news of this made for a very sleepless night. The next morning, after breakfast, they both appeared at the foot of my bed, looking very concerned and serious. After the good morning amenities, they both got down to business and started explaining the changes coming.

These changes started today, including my IV solution and my liquid diet. They were also supplementing some changes to my medication. All these changes were implemented to help control my weight loss rate. They explained to me if I continue to lose weight at this pace, it could cause some very serious complications down the road. Their medical concerns also had me worried about my total recovery.

The doctor took a pause and then shouted out that they had some more good news and bad news, which do I want to hear first. I told him that in all these months, I was getting used to bad news so he could start with that. He said my stay here at the hospital would be much longer than I originally thought. He finished by saying the good news is I wouldn't be returning to the country of Vietnam.

Suddenly, a huge smile came across my face that could only be removed surgically. I thanked them, and said they had just made this the happiest day of my life. They both smiled back at me and said we all have a lot of work to do in getting you back on the road of recovery.

Before they both left my bedside, I told them that the stomach pains and cramps were subsiding a little and asked if I could walk around in my ward. Just as they were about to leave, the doctor shouted back that he would make my request another change starting today.

Until now, my morning routine after breakfast was washing, shaving, and brushing my teeth. I insisted from day one, even as sick as I was, to bathe and shave myself and allow an orderly to keep my hair trimmed. This part of my morning would remain the same, but the latter part of the day would change due to my walking privileges.

I was still smiling and excited about all the new changes, especially the news about not returning to Vietnam. The next thing on my agenda was to let everyone back home share this good news. This would mean sending out several postcards in the next few days.

I felt almost like I was being born again and had the rest of my life to look forward to. Although I was rejoicing out loud, my inner thoughts were sorrowful for all my friends I left back in the jungle, knowing that I would never see them again or know their fate. It left an empty feeling in my stomach. I was sure this wouldn't be the only time in my life that I would think of the friends I left behind and wonder if they ever made it home safe to their loved ones.

Since I was allowed to walk around in my ward, with the exclusion of the bathrooms, my daily routine changed immensely. I could walk to visit other patients, look out different windows and visit the recreation room to watch T.V. It felt like I was starting to live again. This routine was followed for about two weeks before I received better news.

Chapter XXIV

HEADING HOME

There was one significant difference during this flight back to the United States of America; I would enter my country just the same way that I left it, standing up proudly. It would be a long flight with a shortstop in Alaska. Even though I was going to another hospital, it was at least back in the United States. This would be my seventh hospital in about 5 1/2 months.

During my total hospital stay until now, I have lost a total weight loss of 63 lbs. I regained 5 lbs. during the last two weeks before leaving Japan.

My flight had a two-hour stop in Anchorage, AK, for refueling, at which time I was allowed to walk and browse around the airport. The flight continued shortly, and my next stop would be at a field hospital in Oakland, CA. Once I got settled in my new hospital ward, it was time to meet my medical team.

The first thing my new doctor wanted to know was what problems I was having at the present moment. I told him that I was feeling tired, exhausted, and very weak because of all the weight loss. The pains in my stomach had almost subsided and left an uneasy feeling in my abdominal area.

The doctor interjected by saying they would perform numerous tests within the next week, and then he would let me know what was going on. He started to walk away and turned around and said welcome home. He would never know how much those few words meant to me.

It wasn't exactly home, but it was the closest I'd been in almost a year. Already I was thinking of finally being home for the holidays. It was in the middle of September when I entered the Oakland field hospital, and I at least knew I would be spending a week here taking several tests and blood work.

I was so thankful then, just being back in America and eating solid American food. I was anxious to start putting some weight on and feeling like my old self again. At the beginning of the following week, my doctor approached me again with more bad news. It seemed they found an infection in my bowels, and he stated that it would have to be removed surgically.

I expressed great concern about this operation while the doctor assured me that it would be painless, and they wouldn't even have to cut me open. I was astonished and confused when the doctor started explaining the procedure.

He started by saying that they would insert a small metal egg shape object connected to a small plastic hose down my throat; inside this egg was a hook-shaped metal blade. Once this egg was positioned in the right area, it would open, allowing the blade to eject outward. This was all made possible by hooking the end of the plastic tube to a compressor. The blade would then cut out the infected piece and return it to the metal egg.

Once this was accomplished, the tube and egg would slowly be worked back up through the throat. This procedure would take several hours and many X-rays to ensure the egg was in the proper spot. The doctor was correct about being a painless procedure, but it was very uncomfortable. Working the egg back up through the throat was highly unpleasant.

A few days later, I was called to my doctor's office, which I thought was odd. He wanted to explain the results of my surgical procedure with the egg. He informed me that everything went as planned, and they got all the infection. He pointed to a small bottle of liquid with something floating inside that was sitting on his desk.

He said the object inside the tube was a piece of my bowels that they had cut out. He wanted to know if I wanted it for a souvenir. I hesitated for a few seconds and kindly rejected his offer. He smiled while picking up the bottle and dropped it into his wastebasket.

I can't explain the kind of feeling I had at that moment, but it certainly was one of disappointment. I was almost ready to ask him to retrieve the bottle from his wastebasket, but I thought I would be too embarrassed. I thought I didn't have to worry about dying every day, but instead started thinking about living every day. I had to adjust my thoughts from possibly never getting home to the fact I was home and needed to make the proper preparations.

Most of the patients I was mingling with had never been to war and knew little about what was happening in Vietnam. With the thoughts and mindset of my fellow patients, I knew I had a lot of adjusting to do and getting back to my usual way of life.

All my hours awake were thoughts of being home with family and loved ones. I knew I had an uphill battle even after leaving the hospital. Considering all I'd been through in the last six months; I figured I could easily handle it no matter what life would throw at me.

At present, I was only having minor problems with my stomach that the doctors were concerned about. It was the fact that immediately after a meal, the food would pass through me without being properly digested. This problem lasted another week before I received news of another hospital transfer. At least this hospital move would be less than an hour away, into a more extensive facility in San Francisco. I hoped this would be my last hospital move before returning home.

Chapter XXV

SAN FRANCISCO HOSPITAL

It was towards the end of October when I entered the hospital in San Francisco. I was also informed this would be my last hospital before my final discharge and on my way home. The doctors told me they were going to run some final tests and try to determine why I wasn't digesting my food properly. My main problem was shortly after eating, I immediately had to use the bathroom. I couldn't hold the food in my stomach very long, and when discharged, it wasn't digested fully.

For better than a week, when I would use the bathroom, I had to collect a stool sample so it could be analyzed. After that, for a short while, when using the toilet, I wasn't allowed to flush it before it was observed by a nurse on duty.

That was starting to form a habit which to me was terribly troublesome. I noticed that after a meal, within thirty minutes, I was looking for a bathroom. My immediate activities after a meal were limited because I had to stay relatively close to a restroom.

This new hospital was called Letterman General Hospital; it consisted of several floors and numerous elevators.

I had a full roam of the hospital between meal times and tests they performed on me. I just had to sign the book when leaving and resign the same one on my return. On one of my hospital ventures, I was looking out the window and saw the Golden Gate Bridge. I also noticed a general store on one of the floors. I went in to look because I still had no money.

My personal belongings and pay records had never caught up to me during all my hospital travels. I knew that when I finally got discharged, I would get all my back pay for the last year, and everything owed. The problem was that I needed a few dollars to buy some personal items I wanted now. I asked my nurse where to get a small loan until I got my back pay.

The nurse advised me to go to the Red Cross, located on the upper floor of the hospital, and they could help me. I was excited and looking forward to finally having a few dollars in my pocket after a year. The next day I headed to the Red Cross office and eventually saw someone after more than an hour's wait. A heavyset, elderly woman was sitting behind the desk, asking me why I was there.

I started telling her my entire situation, and she stopped me after about twenty minutes and asked me what I would buy with the fifty dollars I wanted from the Red Cross. I told her my list of items like soap, shaving lotion, deodorant, cologne, toothpaste, and various toiletries.

Her answer to me on every item I mentioned was that they were either considered a luxury or just items of want that were not looked at as a need. She then stood up and told me at this time, she would have to deny my request.

I was feeling hurt and dejected. I also stood up and told her she could take that $50 and stick it up her fat ass. I immediately turned around and walked out the door before she could reply. Sadly, and slowly, I started walking back to my hospital ward. When I entered my ward, I saw an Army Lieutenant standing at the foot of my bed.

He immediately asked me if I just left the Red Cross office, and my quick answer was yes, Sir. At that point, I thought I was in big trouble. He wanted to hear my side of the story. I told him all that went on in the office and what I was asking for; I was shocked at his response.

He wanted to know again the amount of money I requested, and I told him fifty dollars. He then reached into his wallet and handed me a fifty-dollar bill. He explained that this was only a loan until I got my back pay. He made sure I knew where his office was in the hospital and said he expected me to pay him back as a soldier and a gentleman.

I assured him that he would be the first person I would look for when I got paid. While I was saluting and thanking him, he started to walk away, then turned around and hollered back at me and said stay away from the Red Cross office. I took his advice, along with his fifty dollars, back to the general store in the hospital to fill my want list. I may have even purchased a few more items that weren't on my original list. I felt like a kid in a candy store that had just found some money on the street.

That quick shopping spree reminded me of Christmas, even though Thanksgiving was only a few weeks away. I didn't mind terribly that I was spending another Turkey Day away from home, but I was determined to be home for the Christmas holidays.

I kept hinting to all my nurses and doctors about being with my family and loved ones during Christmas. They all replied the same; it would depend on my test results. The test and X-rays for my bowel infection all returned negative, meaning they got all the infection from the operation. All my blood tests were returning almost normal, with nothing major to worry about.

Overall, I felt the best I had felt in almost seven months. I continued to have the problem of being unable to digest my food properly and maintaining it in my stomach at any time. After all, I've been through; I didn't look at this issue as a huge problem. It would take some time to cure itself, and I would be able to deal with it.

Since Thanksgiving was only a few days away, I was worried about getting home for the holidays. By now, I was almost hounding my nurses and doctors every day, wanting to know the delay in my discharge back to civilian life. All their answers were the same; the hospital staff was trying to determine the percentage of disability upon my leaving military service.

I was hearing rumors that the percentage of disability was anywhere from ten to forty percent, which to me seemed unimportant at the time. Being home finally for Christmas was the most important thing on my mind. My medical staff informed me that all my tests were over, and they also were waiting for news about my discharge and information concerning my medical follow-up.

It was now Thanksgiving, and I was pleading with my doctor that I would do whatever it took to go home. He told me that he would talk to the hospital commander tomorrow and get back to me as soon as possible.

Two days later, my doctor made an appointment for me to be interviewed by the hospital commander. This meeting lasted for about an hour. It consisted of concerns about my present condition and the immediate future. He also admitted that part of the delay was determining the correct percentage of disability the hospital would offer me.

I quickly interrupted him by asking what I now know was a stupid question. I said, Sir, what if I waived all my disabilities? Would that speed up my discharge? He looked puzzled and paused momentarily, almost like he couldn't believe what he was hearing.

He then asked me to repeat what I just stated so he could make sure he understood me correctly. I did just that, and his answer was did I truly realize what I was saying, and I assured him I did. The tone of his voice instantly changed, and he became very authoritative. He said, young man, if that is your final decision, I could have the proper papers ready for you to review and sign in a few days. Once all that is completed, we will start working on your discharge.

Excitingly, I asked him to give me a time frame for all this to happen, and he answered if all went well, I could be a civilian within a week. He let me know that our meeting was done for now, and when the paperwork gets typed up, he will send for me then. During our departure, he shouted to me that now I could start thinking about going home.

That was the best news I've heard in over seven months. When I finally got back to my ward, and while sitting on my bed, I wondered only for a few seconds if I was making a wise decision. Only time would be the answer to that question, and for now, all my thoughts were on preparing myself mentally for going home. I also knew I had much readjusting, especially with what I had gone through in the past year.

Three days later, I was recalled to the commander's office to review all the paperwork. While I was reading, I truly didn't understand all the legal analogies except I was waiving all my disability rights. The commander did tell me to take my time and read it carefully, and if I had any questions to ask him. The paperwork only consisted of two pages; I'm sure I read it twice.

Being excited and eager to get things going, my only question was, where do I sign? I remember being very nervous while signing the paperwork, but I can't remember ever receiving a copy. From then until now, I regret signing these papers over the years at least 1000 times.

On many occasions, I tried to justify my signing and just what was the makeup of that decision. I had many things to blame it on, such as being young, hospitalized for over seven months, fresh from a war zone, absent from family and loved ones for over a year, and not being in a proper frame of mind.

Also, the fact that I thought about dying every single day for over six months probably clouded my better judgment in that decision. The following day, a Sergeant came to my bedside to take my measurements for a new uniform for my discharge. He explained that they would have accumulated all my final paperwork and backpay for the year in a few days.

The big day had finally arrived, and I was informed that tomorrow I would be receiving my discharge and walking papers and becoming a private citizen once again. I was given my new uniform to try on and wear for the ceremony. I was almost thirty pounds lighter leaving the Army than when I entered.

I spent the entire day and the evening arranging and packing all my belongings. It's not hard to understand the lack of sleep I got during the night. On the big morning, I was showered, dressed, fed, and waiting for someone to come and get me to go to my ceremony.

The festivities were short and sweet, especially when they gave me all my back pay. Before I left the hospital, they also advised me to turn most of the money into travelers' checks, to which I agreed. They gave me all my follow-up papers and thanked me for my service.

They also let me know if I had any more problems from my previous condition, I could go to my nearest VA hospital. Their last words to me were, you are now a free man. I saluted, thanked them all, and said now, let me get on with my life. The first thing in order at the hospital was to return the fifty dollars the Lieutenant loaned me from the Red Cross incident. The second was to transfer most of my back pay into traveler's checks. Next was to visit San Francisco for one day before returning home. It was now December 1st, 1966, and the first day of the rest of my life.

Chapter XXVI

A DAY OF CELEBRATION

During my entire stay at Letterman's Hospital in San Francisco, I became friends with the soldier in the bed next to me. He was in his mid-thirties and a career soldier. We exchange stories and experiences for weeks, day and night. He had some chronic illness that would put him in the hospital at least every few years.

I explained that I was getting discharged soon, and he was my only friend in the hospital and San Francisco. I was telling him that I was going to celebrate, and I would like him to join me entirely at my expense.

We had everything arranged before my day of discharge, and he could get an overnight pass from the hospital if he returned by 5:00 the following day. The plan was that I would go into town close by, get a motel for the night and return around noon to pick him up in the cab. At least I was going to party in the town and wouldn't be alone. When we finished celebrating, we intended to get something to eat before returning to the motel. I promised to take him back to the hospital before his curfew.

Earlier in the day, I made all my telephone contacts back home and alerted everyone of my approximate arrival time the following day. It sounded like another celebration was in the making back home.

Shortly after lunch, I finally picked up my friend at the hospital to start my celebration. I figured wherever we wanted to go, I would call a taxi because neither of us had a car. I now had the money, but not the time to buy an exchange of clothes. I was intending to wear my uniform until I arrived home.

Since I've been absent from the country and away from the media for over a year, I was unaware of the sentiment about the Vietnam War in our country. It seemed that the sight of my uniform during the day and evening antagonized several people, as they were spitting at me and calling me vulgar names. I was called a baby killer and a murderer, along with some insinuations I won't mention here.

I was in total shock and felt sorry for my Army friend, who was dressed in civilian clothes. Even while we were walking down the street, I was getting finger and arm gestures that could have been more friendly. When we would stop to have an occasional drink to celebrate, several people would refuse to have a drink with us, even though I was buying.

I didn't know what to think about this type of reaction because it wasn't what I expected. It's not that I was looking for a hero's welcome or even a pat on the back for a job well done, but a simple thank you would have been sufficient. I let my friend know I was getting a little hungry, but I was afraid to order any food for fear of what they might do to it.

I wondered if my hometown in Niagara Falls, NY, was experiencing the same atmosphere. By now, I couldn't wait to get out of my uniform. During the night, we had a few drinks at various places along the strip, and I was determined to have a good time regardless of the attitude we encountered.

The people with bad attitudes were outnumbered by those willing to talk to us and enjoy our company. Sometime later in the evening, a few people invited us to a house party for a nightcap in appreciation for our service. They gave us their address as they were about to leave and said they would be waiting for us. They also explained it was only two blocks down the street and on the second floor.

We finished our drink and headed for the address. Once we reached it, we headed upstairs to the second floor and knocked on the door. That was the last thing that both of us remembered. We got ambushed from behind. We were knocked out, robbed, and kicked around. The only thing they left in my pocket was the key to my motel. Lucky for that because it had the name of the motel and the address.

Someone called the cab instead of the policeman to get us both back to our motel. I never remember talking to the cab driver, but the woman who owned the motel filled in the rest of the story the following morning. She began by saying it was after 3:00 AM when the cab pulled in, asking for assistance to get us to our room. The night manager helped the cab driver get us to our room on the second floor.

The motel owner went on to say we were both badly bruised and shaken, along with being very drowsy. According to her, I refused all medical attention and police assistance. She also stated that the cab driver wouldn't take any money for the ride or his help. He told her it was his way of showing gratitude for all I did in Vietnam.

I informed the owner I would get cleaned up, take my friend for breakfast, and then return him to the hospital to meet his curfew. I paid for another day because of the incident last night. My plans to return home will be delayed by one day.

My new plan was to go shopping and buy a couple of changes of clothes to prevent a repeat of last night's constant occurrences. I could also use an extra day to heal and lick my wounds. I needed extra free time to indulge in serious meditation about my future. At this point, I was relieved that I only took out a few hundred to celebrate last night in cash while leaving all my checks safely back at the motel.

I wasn't expecting a ticker tape parade on my return home, but getting mugged and robbed the first day I became a free man was the farthest thing on my mind. I got my good friend back to the hospital on time and gave him my sincere apology for all that happened the day before. He also thanked me for our friendship during my stay in the hospital, along with all the generosity I showed him yesterday. We exchange names, numbers, and addresses. Even until this very day, I never heard from him again.

Once back at the motel, I changed my flight and made proper phone calls home. I used the excuse that I needed to shop for clothes without telling them why. Until this very day, I've never whispered this shameful story to a living soul.

Chapter XXVII

GETTING MY LIFE READJUSTED

On returning home, I had a whole mental list of priorities and had to put them in their proper perspective. First and utmost on the list was getting reunited with family and loved ones and becoming reacquainted. The Second was to report to my old job at the DuPont Company and decide on returning date. I had an obligation to check in with the company upon my release from the Army. Once all this was completed, I would take some time off to adjust to civilian life.

After a few short days at home, I felt it would be much harder to get readjusted than I thought. My employer gave me two weeks to report back to work, as I readily agreed it would be sufficient time, but now I had second thoughts about that.

I was enjoying my fiancée, her two young children, and our newborn little boy, who was born while I was in Vietnam. We now have two boys and a girl and were looking forward to a wedding date. We held off on the wedding plans, fearing that I wouldn't return from Vietnam. Everything on the home front seemed to be working smoothly because we'd both been absent from each other for over a year.

It was all my other surroundings and friends that were alienating me. A few of my old friends had told me I wasn't the same person they used to know. I couldn't help noticing that they weren't as eager to get together anytime soon after my initial contact with family or friends. They told me that I was difficult to converse with and seemed withdrawn. I was told I wasn't looking people in the eye when talking, making them uneasy.

I wouldn't allow anyone to ask me questions about Vietnam, and when it did happen, I would answer I didn't want to talk about it. During my seven months in the hospital, I had so many medical problems that nobody ever asked me about my dreams and nightmares. I just assumed that they would go away in time. I also never discussed this problem with anyone since I've been home.

Tomorrow I was reporting back to work and excited about it. I knew the money would be necessary to raise my young family. The first day back on the job was spent looking around and getting reacquainted with the plant areas. After lunch, I was introduced to my new boss to explain and show me around my new job. This took up the complete afternoon, and when he was finished, he said I was done for the day. He said to show up at 8:00 AM with my work clothes.

I answered him back that I was wearing my work clothes. He didn't have another answer but just shook his head, turned, and walked away. For my work clothes, I bought all regular street clothes and took an extra set to work to change when they got dirty. The next morning that was exactly what I reported to work in, and I put my clean set in my locker.

I could see the disgusting look on my foreman's face when I showed up for work with clean street clothes. He assigned me to a group of men, and instantly, I knew I would get the dirtiest job of the day. I planned to do whatever job they gave me, and during my lunch hour, I would shower, change clothes, and return to work. The first time this happened, they all were stunned and lost for words. This type of conduct I would continue until the day I quit.

I was constantly transferred from one department to another. I was considered around the plant as a shit disturber and a troublemaker. After all the gloom and despair on my various jobs, I finally came to one conclusion: I didn't like taking orders anymore. At least I had encouragement on the home front, as my fiancé was making wedding plans and wanted us to be a family forever.

When I first got home, I purchased a brand new 1966 Blue Mustang, and now my fiancé was hinting that it was too small to be a family car. I thought about it, and she was right. Eventually, I would trade my dream car for a more practical family car. I finally traded it in on a ten-passenger station wagon. While increasing my wedding plans, my circle of close friends was decreasing. I hoped it was because of my plans for marriage and not my so-called Vietnam attitude.

At this point, it didn't matter. We were leaving for a week of fun in Vegas and getting married. When we returned from Las Vegas, my wife Patricia and I had only one immediate goal: to care for our family.

I tolerated my job and employers at DuPont for the next several years because the family needed the money. Every day was a challenge at work, and I'm sure I was putting some pressure on them with my attitude that I didn't give a shit about them or the job. I must admit that I was struggling to adjust to civilian life. I constantly had flashbacks to Vietnam during the day and still had nightmares at night.

By working shift work, I would ease some tensions and possibly help with my sleeping. I had no idea what effect it would have on the family. I soon bid on the shift job that included working days, afternoons, and midnights. I got the job the following week and started by working the midnight shift. I was working shift work for the next few years only to discover it wasn't helping my problem.

About a year later, DuPont went on strike, and the rumor was that it would be long. Within the next few days, the company brought busloads of scab workers to take over our jobs. I immediately got a part-time job tending bar at a local Tavern close to my home. I couldn't help thinking that this might be my opportunity to change jobs. I had over nine years with the company and only needed a few months to get my vested rights for retirement.

This was a big decision, but I decided to look for another permanent career during the strike. The fact that I didn't like to get dirty on the job or even work hard enough to work up a sweat had something to do with my next career. I decided to enter sales as an independent salesman. This would allow me to wear a suit every day and only work as hard and long as I wanted.

The fact that I would be my own boss was a definite plus, as I had a problem with authority. I'm sure all these qualities are related to the Vietnam debacle. Once again, I gave up all my retirement rights because I refused to return to my old job for a few months.

I would continue in total commission sales with the LaSalle Extension University and The Independent Order of Foresters for a few years each. Finally, I purchased my restaurant and tavern and continued with that until my retirement. I published my first book last year about my endeavors over the thirty-five years of its existence, and that title is "It's Not Easy Being Me, Bar Hopping Thru Life."

Chapter XXVIII

DIAGNOSED WITH PTSD

It's been almost forty years since my Vietnam War experience, and until this very day, I have never talked about it with a living soul. All this time, I thought I had locked up all those thoughts in my brain like a steel box. Every so often, something would happen during the day, and like a key, it would open that box and let all these horrible thoughts come tumbling out.

I knew my behavior would change, and most of the time, it wasn't for the better. I would become distant and withdrawn from the people around me, especially those closest to me. It would take great effort to get all those thoughts locked back in that steel box again. While these thoughts were loose from the box, I was somewhat troubled inside, but little did I know I was hurting the people around me at the time. This usually entailed family, loved ones, and close friends.

In 2005, I was retiring, selling my business, and getting divorced for the second time. It was a busy year. When all these three things were accomplished, I was headed to Myrtle Beach,

SC, to live out my remaining years by the ocean. I had to see a doctor several times before I established any medical insurance. Each time this occurred, I would pay the full price in cash out of my pocket.

One day, I was talking to my neighbor about my insurance problem, and he answered my dilemma. He knew I was a veteran and advised me to take my discharge papers, go to the Myrtle Beach VA Clinic, and register into the system. Once I was registered with the Veterans Administration, I was getting all my medical problems solved with just a small copay. I was told I could have received this kind of benefit for the past forty years. I couldn't believe the thousands of dollars I could have saved in medical bills and monthly insurance premiums for all those years.

Once again, all the benefits I had coming to me were never explained during my discharge from the hospital. Myrtle Beach had an in and outpatient clinic, but it needed to be more extensive in the services it offered. Most medical care was done in Charleston, SC, about one hundred miles away. Since I didn't have a car at the time for all my appointments, I had to take the VA shuttle bus. These appointments would take all day because the bus usually carries up to twelve other patients. I made these appointments regularly for six years, during which most of my medical problems were connected to my service in the Army.

2011 at one of my appointments, I was diagnosed with stage 4 throat and tongue cancer. This was a life-threatening situation. The doctors told me the tumor was so large in my throat that they were amazed I could still swallow any food. I was immediately assigned to a team of cancer specialists and surgeons to determine the best type of treatment for this cancer.

After weeks of studies and tests, they decided to give me the ultimate amount of radiation and chemotherapy that the body could endure for six weeks, along with excessive medications. During all this preparation, I was informed that stage 4 cancer was an extremely advanced stage. This, of course, didn't make me feel any better.

I could read between the lines from talking to my doctor and support team over the weeks that my survival would be a long shot. Halfway through my treatments, I was losing much weight and getting weaker by the day. I also lost my voice due to all the radiation daily in my throat. I had to carry a pen and pad to write down while trying to communicate with people.

It was at this point I was convinced that my life was coming to an end. I decided to write a journal about my life and war experiences. I wanted my family, loved ones, children, grandchildren, and great-grandchildren to understand better what kind of man I was. Every night I would write a few pages, which turned into chapters. I prayed daily that I would live long enough to finish my two journals; sometimes, I had serious doubts.

During my many trips to Charleston during my cancer treatments, a volunteer shuttle bus driver requested to talk to me. He wanted to buy me lunch, but I settled for coffee.

He explained that he observed me on numerous trips to Charleston and wanted to know if I was a Vietnam veteran. I answered yes, and he wanted to know if I was in the infantry. My answer, again, was affirmative, and he started asking me all sorts of questions about my time in the service. We were both pressed for time, so we exchanged numbers, as he insisted on calling me soon.

It was about two weeks when I got his call, and he wanted to take me to meet a medical advisor about my service. I refused his offer, and he said he would call me back later. About another week passed before he called again, and I finally accepted his offer to meet this advisor.

The meeting lasted about an hour, and I was informed that I probably suffered from PTSD. After the meeting with the medical advisor, I was scheduled to meet with various doctors and readjustment counselors. For the next few months, I remained busy with numerous appointments testing me for PTSD. Until now, I never heard of the term or knew its meaning.

Finally, I was sent to Charleston VA Hospital for a session with their psychiatrist. His final observation and opinion were I had been suffering from PTSD disorder ever since my Vietnam days. Between my team of doctors and counselors, all recommended group counseling along with medication prescribed by my psychiatrist. This treatment method lasted six years until I had problems with some group members. At that time, I was suggested to leave the group and join an anger management class. I started the class the following week, lasting for eight weeks. I enjoyed the class and took another eight-week advanced anger management class. In both classes, when finishing, I was presented with a certificate of achievement.

During my therapy treatment, I also took medication from my psychiatrist four times a day and visited every three months. The government was still testing for my other ailments connected to my service. I was being treated for my feet, stomach, ears, and eyes, along with my PTSD.

My cancer by now was in remission, but I was being seen by my team of doctors every few months. Once again, the government decided to give me another percentage of disability, adding up to over 150%. They finally agreed to give me 100% for the rest of my life.

I am currently seeing all my disability doctors, including my psychiatrist, regularly. I am also seeing my readjustment counselor once a month. I have to admit, it was painful rewriting this book from my war journals, but since I have been very accustomed to pain, I felt it was just something I had to do.

On my left is Larry Eldridge(Shuttle Driver), myself Larry Delong center and Donnie Oaks on my right.